THREADS BEYOND THE TEXT

City Brick Reader's Guide: How Fascinating Tools and Techniques Of Creative Writing Made A Dynamic Memoir

M. Catherine Bunton

ISBN: 979-8-9936706-1-4

Edited by James R. Sodon

Published 2026 by
City Brick
Saint Louis, Missouri

Dedication

To those creative writers who walk the high wire of scrutiny, and of "What will they think?" You risk the chance of a fall, but a safe landing brings profound satisfaction. Bless you for every step you take.

Acknowledgements

My thanks to Jim Sodon my trusted editor and friend, Maria Thomas who brought the Brick Palace into the world of art. Much appreciation to the readers of the City Brick Series who are standing by for more inspiration that comes when stardust words align in new and creative ways. And to Greg, always Greg.

The Author's Opening Number

Threads Beyond The Text is about the dynamic kickoff book of my memoir, *The Shelter of Trees*. *Threads* is a spy glass to look deeper between the leaves at the limbs and trunks of the trees, the structural, bare bones of a story that continues to unfold.

Inside are the same four characters who narrated the history of a city that made magic by using stardust clay to make perfect brick. Take a peek at the process and the poetry that became a recipe for family fun, and fantasy.

This companion book exposes the tree roots that led to Books II – V: *The Shelter of Cool Confidence, Paper The Moon With Stardust Words, The Stardust Kingdom Trail,* and *The Shelter of City Brick*. My Opening Number is a plea to write with me, but first

Try Listening To The Trees

Feel the spirit of the breeze that runs through the trees as the Chorus sings of their glory

Hear them talk as Cleve takes a walk, and tells their incredible story

Have faith in a tree, and in what you can't see, for maybe it's really there

Table of Contents

A Welcome Letter

Dear Readers, Teachers, and Group Leaders,

Welcome to The Reader's Guide for Book I of the City Brick Memoir Series. Whether you're leading a classroom discussion, hosting a book club, or just seeking inspiration to write for enjoyment, this guide invites you to explore The City Brick Memoir Series. It offers historical fiction, a little fantasy, a little humor, and more than a lot of imagination.

Having taught creative writing for many years at two Community Colleges, I've written this guide to spark the interest of those who seek new examples of how to write creatively.

This companion book brings a whole new angle to Book I of the series, The Shelter of Trees. It offers interactive discussions that bring new perspectives and inquiries to the story. Readers are encouraged to talk back, talk up, and write responses to the new ideas generated.

Just like each book in the series, this companion provides space for reflection, rethinking, and review of the rather non-traditional story elements. Review being quintessential to learning, these pages bring yet another opportunity to get a fresh look at writing techniques that:

1. *Prompt discussion*
2. *Add to the reader's understanding of creative writing.*
3. *Cross genres of writing instruction, humor, history, and fiction.*
4. *Encourage journaling of personal comments about new ideas.*

Whether you are a literary junkie, student, teacher, or a seeker of something new and different, these stardust words might be just what you are looking for. I hope they inspire your own stardust words and light the spark of your imagination.

I remain,

M. Catherine Bunton

A Walk Outside Myself
Into Historical Fiction

Discussing *The Shelter of Trees* in a play format is to experience the events of the book in a new way. One of the narrators, Cleve, said it in his own way on page 28, “I’ve always felt that a story is a walk you take with its author. You stroll along a mystic street where your imagination folds into the author’s imagination and you both are spirited away, It’s like you take a brisk out-of-body expedition. Oh the joys of walking through a story.”

So we will walk again through the story, this time on stage. We have treaded the tail of a comet as we tried to keep up with Myay. Yes, the comet, as you can imagine is the wonder child Myay. Now it’s time to take a seat, pull out the spy glasses and get a close-up view of how the story plays out on a stage.

The cast members all have their own backstory. We’ll start with the author, yes I’m in the play. So we have the Malones and the Kielys, my gracious family who cared for each other and the sweet neighbors. Also, and this is where it gets interesting, there are virtual characters. I believe I found them, or created them, as pieces of myself that were waiting to emerge from the heaps and piles of clay and stardust of which I am made. So began their literary lives, and they have been of the greatest assistance in relating the events associated with the legacy of an original Star Girl. It will be your job to figure out who that is.

The author's family, the Malones and Kielys are characters who, if they were still alive would be prime time protagonists in stories of Old North St. Louis. They are now part of a large group I've entitled The Disadvantaged Royalty. These fine people toiled in a variety of professions like laborers, bricklayers, street workers, and so many others but required absolutely no fame for it. I thank them every day, maybe twice.

These Disadvantaged Royalty, the Malones and Kielys, are vibrant and alive in my memory as kind, courageous, and joyful angels who are somewhere in the spirit world waiting for me. I hope my words come just a little close to reflecting the depth and the warmth of their love.

It's early, but let's go back, or recap if you will, it's the way to give you a satisfying read. Personally, I hate it when I'm confused by a bunch of characters right off the bat, so let's take it nice and easy. We have a multi-pronged storyline to deal with. I find it intensely interesting but if you're not paying attention it will slip through the cracks of your understanding,

One plot line is the antics of our little girl, Myay. She is a corker, always waiting for another fish to fry, or at least a fried bologna sandwich to inhale. Another idea running through the text is that Myay is one of four pieces of me who emerged in the series. The quartet that is the brain trust and essence of most of my dialogue shakes out like this. Myay is the child in me, Iris is her older self. Cleve is sort of my alter-ego, but I've called him a lot of things so the jury's still out really. And The Writer is a kind of overseer who tries to keep everyone on track.

A third storyline is the fact that these virtual pieces of myself are as real as the Knowing Trees of Jennings who populate the streets and know more than they should. The final storyline is that of two domiciles, Myay's house in Jennings and her aunt's red brick sanctuary in North St. Louis. Here's the synthesizer that pulls it all together: the author's family, the characters inside her, the neighbors and trees and houses are all made of stardust. It might be the main plot that runs deep throughout the storylines.

This stardust is the treasure in Treasure Island, the Philosopher's Stone of Harry Potter fame, the Holy Grail of everything I write. Big reveal, in case you didn't catch it in the series, it was in the brick that built North St. Louis. If that's not creative enough for you, you probably won't want to follow along with me through the literary techniques that built this multi sub-personae plot.

But if you do, you will discover that most everything I write is based on the premise that this glorious stardust is in all things, especially the four pieces of me, the virtual characters you met and learned to love throughout the series. They hate when I call them virtual. However, stardust is the catalyst inside my stardust words, and these not-so-virtual characters believe it is stardust that makes them tick.

I happen to know they are right. Almost every element in our human bodies was forged inside a star. It's been important to the series for readers to understand that stardust elements were in the very clay of St. Louis soil which, by the way, made for the most exquisite brick anywhere in the country.

Stardust formed the first light and illuminated the entire universe, an eternally good life source for all of us who exist here. As descendants of the stars, we then are part of the original catalyst for all that is good. A lifelong journey to keep it in our sights could get us up there among the stars in The Land of Goodness and Joy.

Was this Myay's journey as she trekked through the stardust mud of her backyard and through stardust words on the trail to her aunt's Palace of Brick? Her journey is the same one we're all on. We seek to know how the miracle of such goodness got here and then got inside us. I believe the stardust in us is what breeds a divine and abiding goodness in our heart that I call our Stardust Chamber.

You'll remember that later in the series Myay reaches the Land of Goodness and Joy by staying on the stardust trail. And yes, it helped to have messages laid out for her that were written by the stars. You may also remember from Book IV, page 54, that the second message written in starlight was that: "the gift of stardust elements in your blood comes with a responsibility to let others know they have it too." You know, the stars are straight shooters and their advice draws crowds.

If we follow the light of the stars, we can spread the news that the stars bring each night when they shine. We can rekindle the virtue of respect for our neighbors, the kind of respect we saw from Myay's kind neighbors of Jennings. They were "real" neighbors who gave a helping hand when needed and made the neighborhoods of the 50s work so well for society.

The story has dialogue; talking is so healthy especially in books where you have time to digest it. I thought it would be helpful for you to see how I dialogue when I talk to the parts of myself as I write. I'm talking about the four parts of me I introduced you to in the series. Our conversation has turned out to be a pretty creative way to dialogue. Here's how it came about.

I was often tense at my home in Jennings that I call the Hansel and Gretel House of Helen Avenue. Worry in a little girl can bring on chronic anxiety; it's sort of like always feeling as though the sky is falling. I remember one day during a particularly upsetting episode I stood in front of the full length mirror. I looked in the mirror and said to myself, if I could just get out of this body then I wouldn't be upset. But my role at Hansel and Gretel was to love and be loved. I wasn't programed to bail out on my sweet family, not physically, spiritually, or mentally.

I do believe, though, that it was probably anxiety that caused some disassociation in my early attempts to write, because in the mirror I could swear I saw myself walk out of my body and disappear, yet I was still there seeing my reflection. I don't think you can make this stuff up, and I don't think I ever did that at any other time, but that day it did happen. It singed some of my stardust, but you can't keep a stardust seeker down,

That happened when I was Myay. Later when I was Iris and I was writing about the memory of that day, something dawned on me. *I thought wait a minute, I'm writing as Iris who is a part of myself, and I'm writing about Myay who used to be part of myself, and Cleve who is a part of myself that came from nowhere, and The Writer, who is a part too much like me. Why? Who does this? And where is the real me?* It kind of stunned me for a second when I connected writing in this way to the day I walked outside myself on Helen Avenue.

Was there something in my subconscious that broke into pieces that day? I can't say it was my soul because that would be a sacrilege, I think. But what part of me broke? My psyche? My nerves? I actually have no clue. All I know is that I am now aware of it, and maybe fear of being myself affected me when I started writing fiction and creating characters. Then when I started a memoir about me, I suppose the breakup manifested into four narrators that represented the parts of me that split off. Truth being stranger than fiction is not a cliché.

I really never wanted to admit any of this, especially that I was hiding in my writing behind my characters. So, I say in the memoir that the four parts of me emerged due to an overload of love that needed more ways to communicate. That was partly true, and it seemed as good a reason – excuse - as any. I don't know if I'll ever know the real reason why it happened. The upside is I've been living with all four virtuals (sorry) and we get along pretty well. It beats writing alone.

I know, however, there will come a day when I'll have to come to grips with just being me. I think it's close, but I desperately do not want to hurt anyone's feelings, not even the virtual characters of myself. Not wanting to hurt anyone's feelings is why my memoir is written as historical fiction.

The day to fix the split is not here yet, so I carry on and call the four parts of me The Chorus. They want to be your writing companions. When you get to know them, us, me and them, you will find out we are over-achievers. But doesn't everyone want to change the world in a good way? We do. It's just who we are.

Myay, the child in me is probably something like the child in you, the child that never goes away. Myay grows into Iris, a young woman who writes and teaches writing, and probably tries too hard to provide advantages for those who don't have them. Unearthing goodness and spreading it around is a commitment of hers and commitments can be addictive.

There's Cleve, a gentle guardian, I guess, our conscience who lowers the boom on Myay and Iris when their over-achieving requires the brakes to be put on. And the more mature aspect of me is The Writer. She is my enigma, though, with an obsession to find the next idea that might change someone's life. That's all five of us. We're a team and we want to help you ignite the spark of your creative genius. I'm glad the virtuals manifested themselves to help me do that.

The good news is that The Municipal Opera House of St. Louis has been gracious enough to let us use their open air setting, taking out the rows of seats and bringing in tables and chairs to help create a workshop atmosphere. In this setting you are welcome to interact with a script that includes me, our Director, stagehands, and each of the virtual (oops) characters.

Feel free to speak up and ask questions. You are no longer simply a Companion Writer, you are a participant and I'm jumping in too.

Two Houses That Were Nonfiction

The Hansel and Gretel House

In the beginning you'll remember that Cleve, my wise conscience, narrated a walk through Jennings, Missouri, ushering readers along Helen Avenue. I was called Myay by my aunt during the years. Our address was 5250 Helen Avenue. Although there was nothing fictional about the house, I refer to it as the Hansel and Gretel House because it was built of sadness and sweetness too. It was a bit of a shack yes, but a sugar shack.

The other virtual characters eventually walked along with Cleve. They became my trusted writing companions because they were part of me. They never balked when I wrote them into the house of fiction or created their dialogue which, in a way, illuminated their very different personalities. But as I was thinking over the development of a reader's guide for Book I of the series, I began to worry that I shouldn't have written a memoir, I mean all five books, as historical fiction.

The virtual narrators, four hybrid parts of myself who know the most about me are becoming more real. At the time, historical fiction felt like the right genre when they spoke. They told the story of how Myay, sought the way to another very real house, my dear aunt's flat in North St. Louis. My aunt's door, purse, and heart were always open. Her home was truly a safe haven from the tension of the Hansel and Gretel House. It was a respite for me, my mother, sister, and brother Frank.

The journey that began in Book I toward the house in North St. Louis was along a trail paved with stardust words, a whimsical bit of historical fiction. But I was compelled to continue teaching creative writing, so the practical part of me, The Writer, took over. As a result Book II and III just became prose of another color entirely, sort of instructional writing.

I don't think I realized that I was threading my way into text that was less fiction. But I did realize I was losing Myay's thread in the middle of my memoir so I put her back on the trail in Books IV and V.

I thought this rather unusual and disjointed memoir might serve as an example for young writers to proceed with caution. Sometimes the directional signals a writer watches just keep flashing, so proceeding can be perilous. The signals sent me to historical fiction, then started pointing toward nonfictional prose, and then back again to historical fiction. In thinking about a Readers Guide for Book I, *The Shelter of Trees*, well I was getting dizzy.

Hang with me here and know that if you write this kind of stuff happens. I started to write the companion book in the form of a play that would allow me to be a member of the cast. It worked pretty well as I revealed some of the literary devices I used to write the series, and to clear up some of the mystery as to why going to my aunt's was such a relief.

I rolled through three scenes of the play, but started to worry again that it was too much historical fiction. So I looked for another signal and proceeded to re-frame the whole thing as a symposium, but no go. I then re-framed it a third time as a seminar which, I thought, would be a more appropriate format for a reader's guide, but no good again. What happened was I couldn't finish any of those formats, and I guess that was my signal to just stop.

I was terribly stuck and for some time I didn't know why. I told my editor that I would rework the readers guide into a group of essays that would be much more straight forward in its reveal. I created a cover with the title, *The Girl Who Fled From Fiction.* Ugh, too radical! Over time, it felt like the girl at a crossroads, accelerating but not getting anywhere.

I started to question myself again as to why I was being so extreme as to declare a break from fiction, and why I had completely ditched the idea of publishing the play that I had put so much time into.

I began researching a variety of genres and read up on a technique called metafiction which allows a writer to break the fourth wall. Walls being the three sides of the stage and the fourth being the one between the actors and the audience.

Eureka! I thought this is it. This is how I get into the finale and into the outer edges of reality that I'm looking for. By breaking the fourth wall and using metafiction to finish off the play, I was creating a bridge out of my historical fiction into the world of nonfiction while not giving up fiction totally. Whew!

After reworking the finale, I can now step beyond the text of historical fiction with a clear conscience. I can write about the real world I inhabited in the decades after the 50s. These years were blessed because I met my husband Greg. Our life was dominated by love, school, and jobs that built my writing skills.

I am happy to have walked inside the world of historical fiction, and happy also that I found an escape mechanism. I know I can return any time I want to, and that I don't have to leave fiction behind or abandon my beloved characters. Fiction, like Auntie's welcoming shelter in North St. Louis, are two fabulous houses whose characters will always have my loyalty.

I really hope this explanation of my stopping and starting helps readers be aware that there's bumps along any road of creation. I think of creative writing like the game of Pick Up Sticks. You drop ideas on the page and they're all mixed up. You carefully and deliberately start to pick them apart. But you keep looking at the pile that's left and you think, I can't get any more ideas out of the pile, they're just too tangled up. So you stop the game, sit back, and think about it. Then you grab up all the sticks and drop them again. This time the pile doesn't look as intimidating and maybe, just maybe, you can make sense out of them.

So, here's how the sticks straightened themselves out into my original play with a metafiction finale. And a temporary farewell to my virtual characters who built The City Brick Memoir Series.

I hope to end our time together by enjoying each other's company with old fashioned fun, food and spirits. So I'll see you afterwards in the side garden with the string lights at Fuzzies' Friendly Corner.

P.S. If you happen to run into one of my characters don't use the term virtual or metafiction or even fiction. They're getting more sensitive every day.

THREADS BEYOND THE TEXT
CITY BRICK MEMOIR COMPANION
THE SHELTER OF TREES
M. Catherine Bunton
M. CATHERINE BUNTON

Play Contents

A Play In Three Acts
The Shelter of Trees

Epigraph

A piece of creative writing,
like a day dream,
is a continuation of,
and a substitute for,
what was once
the play of childhood.

Sigmund Freud

Storyboard: City Brick Memoir Series

Image	Title	Theme
	The Shelter of Trees	Goodness And Joy
	*The Shelter of Cool Confidence*	Seeking Creativity
	*Paper the Moon with Stardust Words*	Practice Makes Perfect
	*The Star Kingdom Trail*	Mysterious Journey
	*The Shelter of City Brick*	You Are Now Over The Rainbow

Cast of Characters

Humans

Stagehands of St. Louis MO: *young capable men and women with technological, architectural, and artistic talent.*

The Director: *a middle aged man who does the work of three people to keep productions on track. He's stressed but able to enjoy every performance.*

The Author of The City Brick Memoir Series: *A stardust seeker, still striving to reveal how creative writing breaks through the boundaries of imagination to discover new truths.*

The Audience: *a diverse group, curious as to the author's intent in writing a historical fantasy told through multiple, virtual narrators.*

Virtual Characters

The Knowing Trees: *wise as owls and some of the oldest beings on Earth. They communicate through their roots and they know how to protect us, especially these trees.*

The Virtuals: *Myay, Iris, Cleve, and The Writer, members of a group known as the Chorus, or The Trojan Horse when they are performing.*

Are you with me?

AUTHOR'S PRE-SHOW ADDRESS

DIRECTOR

Curtain in Fifteen!

The Author walks on stage into a spotlight and addresses the audience.

AUTHOR

So you want to know the genesis of my City Brick Memoir Series? Really, I do too. Before we begin, though, I want to reiterate some things I'm sure I've said in the past. I've found that if you're going to be good at something, say writing, you can't do it just once and expect to master it.

I've learned the hard way that once is not only not enough, but nowhere near. Learn to enjoy asking yourself questions like, "Hey, does that word make sense there?" "Does this sentence add anything to my story?"

You wouldn't want a microwave or lawn mower or heart monitor that wasn't tested. It's the same with a piece of writing. It's just good to rethink it and find ways to make it work better. News Flash: I bet I edited the five books of my memoir a hundred times and they could still use a going over.

With each book I tried to offer a more complex writing challenge for readers. In this Reader's Guide I hope to offer more information *about* writing, like devices and techniques that you'll want to know about as you compose whatever it is your heart sets out to write.

In this play, I'm inviting you to be part of the script so that I don't talk at you but with you. I'll suggest definitions of some of the literal terms I used, and give you the opportunity to respond. I want to give you novelty, not run of the mill repetition, so that this companion format to *The Shelter of Trees* helps you grow as a creative thinker and writer.

This is a second chance to analyze some of the episodes that make up the first book in the series, *The Shelter of Trees*. I will provide space in this book, as I always do, for you to interact by writing your own editorial comments. And I hope you speak your mind in whatever group in which you are participating.

My own editorial comments are a chance to begin again. That's why I love editing so much. I have written, *The Tree of Beginning Again Grows In St. Louis*. *The Tree of Beginning Again* is in all of us. So think of this companion to *The Shelter of Trees* lets us re-view it with new eyes, and begin to again to understand it in new ways. Are you with me?

Check One:

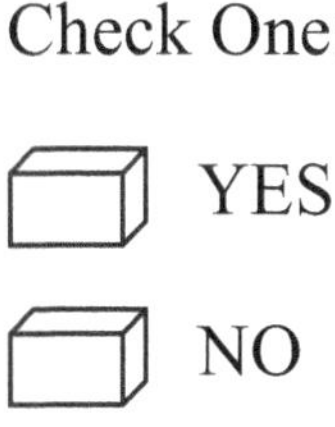
YES

NO

If you're still hearing my words, your first interaction must have been 'YES.' So, I'll proceed with this

Reader's Guide which is a re-vision of the kickoff book in the series. It's a different way of experiencing it. The narrators are the same, but you and I are in the script now.

I've re-framed some events to make them more meaningful. I hope each book offered creative techniques for your own writing, and that this dramatic re-format of Book I offers even more. This re-format is now a workshop to discover what goes on in the story of Myay's stardust trail with its hidden themes and foreshadowing that will now come to light.

The hints to solve the mysterious and veiled rhetorical devices are in the *Threads Beyond the Text,* and I hope you are captured by their allure as you attempt to unravel them. Don't look for help from me. I'm as much in the dark as you are, because somebody was pulling at my threads every time I put fingers to keys.

The story is real, and the virtuals are as real as me. Am I in awe of my own creations? You bet I am. As book II of the series says, "You never know what you think until you see it in ink." And when you do see it, you may be in for a wonderful surprise.

Let's begin again, you and I, in wonder.

THE SHELTER OF TREES
BOOK I
PRESENTS
A THREE ACT PLAY
ON STAGE AT THE MUNY
IN FOREST PARK

DIRECTOR

Places!

Stagehands quietly begin moving cardboard trees into place. The sound of rustling paper fills the air. The Director calls out again:

Quiet on the set!

Lights up on ACT I as the author of the City Brick series re-appears.

ACT I
Scene One
Book I. Pages 6 – 38

AUTHOR

Good afternoon and welcome to the 1950's neighborhood of Jennings, Missouri, and the trees that grew there. Trees are dear to me, and they haven't really changed much since the 50's. In fact, for me they have threads beyond the text of the City Brick Memoir Series. We go back to 2014 with the publication of my children's book series.

As an advocate of lost causes, I wrote about the Assembly of Trees in my children's series with the goal of making our youth aware of the importance of trees and the role they play in the survival of our planet. Although the destruction of trees continues the to this day, I will continue to be their advocate.

I would like to see a global *Day of Trees,* like the Arbor Day we once had. Trees photosynthesize, which they say is simply taking a selfie with the sun. But as they develop their critical snapshots, the process magically makes oxygen like their kin phytoplankton makes it under the ocean.

As trees communicate through their roots, the discussion usually gets around to the fact that we humans take them for granted even though they give us every breath we take. They know their roots are made, in part, of stardust as are all things like the words formed by the breaths we take. Breath and words contain stardust elements of nitrogen and oxygen. I've found no other explanation for the make-up of breath and words.

And like the trees and the stars, and all of life forms, we are rooted in the cosmos. We humans are vessels who consume the nitrogen and oxygen of stardust and of trees. We make breath out of it and form words that lead to understandings. Breath and words, being made, in part, of stardust is one of those understandings I've always believed in.

The universal knowledge that has evolved from the stardust words we breath comes from a place far beyond any text we've ever known. It comes from an always moving vibration of sound in a cosmic corpus that threads along like musical notes into the leaves of trees, making each one a song of its own.

Setting is the physical environment of a story that creates its atmosphere.

So trees will be our setting, although in the book they are more than setting. They are characters just like the virtual characters who narrated the entire memoir series. I don't want them to think I too take them for granted. I now ask for your close attention as the trees have an announcement.

The stagehands are busy connecting the audio wires to the trees' branches so their voices will sound proud and strong. The first tree speaks.

THE FAMILY TREE

Our crisis continues, so we thank you for the opportunity to deliver our message. We like to keep our spirits lighthearted, but this situation is serious. Climate change is affecting our family of trees, and who better to sound the alarm than us? We have tried throughout the ages to protect humanity from the scorching effects of the sun.

Our efforts, however, are even more critical since we have reached a tipping point in the Earth's climate. Many do not want to believe what is happening. We understand. Their disregard is based in fear, fear it might be true that we, their Shelter of Shade, will fail them. It's much easier to dismiss the whole idea and pretend it's not happening.

But we shall continue to engage the children and adult citizens to act in our behalf. There is power in numbers, and jointly we will be better able to control the climate, and calm its extremes.

So, my dear Author, if you want to decipher threads beyond the text, as the title of this reader's guide purports to do, we are elated that you are looking at the threads that run through our leaves. They are the artwork, drawn by nature's invisible hand, in colors and shapes as unique as DNA.

Since you began your writing career with *The Little Maestro* you have featured trees. So we thought you wouldn't mind if we toot our own horn by offering you an epigraph of our own. It's from another who also acknowledges our value.

We Knowing Trees serve as your metaphor for protection in the same way that bricks do later in the series. They edged us out of first place, but we are forgiving as long as we can offer our own quote from a scientist friend of ours who captured what we always knew in our bones and branches:

> "We humans look rather different from a tree. Without a doubt we perceive the world differently than a tree does. But down deep, at the molecular heart of life, the trees and we are essentially identical."
>
> Carl Sagan, *Cosmos*

Thank you Mr. Sagan, and thanks to Cleve who features me on page 9 to be exact. We know that most have a family tree, but none like me. You went to great pains to describe the four parts of yourself; however, I paint a picture that's worth a trunk full of words.

I suppose I'll stop bragging now and pass the baton to an old colleague of mine, The Sagger of Jennings. Yes, the Maple Tree has shaded the Malones and their neighbors for years as they spun tales of their day-to-day lives. And for better or worse, the Maple kept a log.

DIRECTOR

This Companion Book puts *The Shelter of Trees* in a new light, reintroducing characters, explaining literary devices, and prompting questions for discussion. So when I think an extra explanation is needed, I'll have a stagehand carry out a sign, just like the old Vaudeville days.

The Family Tree mentioned being referred to as a metaphor; let's start there. A metaphor is a figure of speech that compares two subjects without the use of the words "like" or "as." Easy peasy.

MAPLE KNOWING TREE

Good to know our Director is hip to the program. Now me, I'm a good listener and known as the Nosy Rosy of Jennings here to do a little house keeping. You will all be given a pad of paper with your program this evening on which to write your thoughts as we tread a little deeper into the fabric of literature. And oh yes, the paper comes to you compliments of the Birch Trees' sturdy paper bark.

PEAR KNOWING TREE

Allow me to branch off into another subject which is botany. Yes, we're more than scenery. We are anchors in the Earth. Our roots grow horizontally and straight down. They make a beautiful pattern like the veins on our leaves. Do forgive the literary reference, but unlike our cousin The Tree of Heaven which grows out of pavement, our roots do reach twelve to eighteen inches deep throughout Jennings. We are deciduous detectives in a way, gathering news for Cleve so he can give the best tours possible.

I've had the advantage of growing in Myay's back yard where the neighbor ladies visited and talked to Myay's mother when they needed a compassionate ear. I testify that the dramatic personae of trees in the book and in this presentation is factually correct. We trees are characters and we have good memories.

Merriam-Webster defines dramatis personae as the characters or actors in a drama.

BIRCH KNOWING TREE

And when we are done, and if we can trust you with small pocket knives, and if you want to, we'll have you come up on stage and carve your initials in our trunks. We may be covered in initials from root to crown by the time our run is over, but we like initials. Why our very roots are carved into the Earth's soil. So we understand the need to be remembered.

St. Louis will be remembered for its trees by thousands of readers who view the covers of the memoir series. The books highlight The Tree of Goodness and Joy, The Tree of Believing In Yourself, The Tree of Creativity, The Tree of Possibility, and The Tree Of Beginning Again. These trees attest to the spirit of St. Louis that thrives in good times and bad, but always endures.

THE CHINESE ELM KNOWING TREE

I'll take it from here. Even though I'm older than most of my colleagues, the trees of Jennings, I'm just about the only tree on Helen Avenue that stands tall in a front yard. I have arthritis of the trunk and severe thinning of the leaves, but know this. I was born on the four foot front lawn of the Malone's Hansel and Gretel House for a reason.

My fate has been to bloom where I was planted, so I gave the Malones a lot of cover. What kind? Well, use your imagination and I'll go rest my limbs.

The audience takes note of that.

THE DIRECTOR

The Chinese Elm just hinted at one of the Author's foreshadowing statements. But, like other intimations, they never come out of the shadows.

Foreshadowing is a literary device whereby the author provides clues as to what will happen later in the story.

The audience takes more notes as the AUTHOR steps into a brighter light. She leans toward the audience and whispers that Myay may not be heard from as often now as she was in the book – her thread seemingly unraveling a bit.

Seriously, this is about
Virtual Characters

and

Stardust.

AUTHOR

Myay's agenda emerged with the most strength in the series, but we have other priorities now. I was fairly restrained as Myay, but at times I could try my dear mother's patience. I wasn't spoiled but often she did address me with, "Hey Lady Jane" which served as an air pump letting the energy out of my next move.

Myay was the CEO at her school's candy counter, writing out inventory sheets for sno-caps and red licorice. But Iris ,the young woman that Myay grew into, she opted for the college classroom and creative writing curriculums. Fate really is the hunter, and the script will definitely follow Iris' thread.

AUTHOR

This play offers scriptogenesis whereby you are changed by assimilating the ideas and messages of the play's script.

In the book, I narrate through several parts of myself, all mostly in the past tense, yet each part still exists in me, a somewhat "author's eye" omniscient narration in a segmented way.

Point of View is the perspective from which a story is narrated as in first person "I," second person "you," and third person "he or she."

It's natural to characterize who you were at various stages of life. I thought it was right to acknowledge those stages by name and give each a voice. But I'm wary. They've gotten a bit smarter than me, like AI purportedly will advance beyond human capacity. My virtual characters, especially Iris, may be waiting to take us humans on. Be not afraid!

The audience murmurs and a man stands to speak.

AUDIENCE MEMBER

I guess we were all different at different stages of our life. So yes, I relate somewhat. But that's a little spooky to me. I can imagine virtual characters gaining on us because we are mortal. They don't die as far as I know.

AUTHOR

Good thought. As a creative writer, the world I'm creating is The Land of Goodness and Joy. It is not exclusive. All ideas are welcome, especially the ones that turn into fictional characters. These characters live at The Story Hotel in the City of Possibility. Now my virtuals live there too. Thanks for kicking off our first broad minded conversation about the possibilities of virtual reality.

Another member of the audience shouts out.

AUDIENCE MEMBER

Yeah! How about writing a guide for *The Shelter of The Story Hotel*? The place must be pretty big.

The audience laughs as if they were thinking the same thing.

AUTHOR

Fair enough. But before Myay and Iris check in there let me say you never know where they might surface again. Myay was the child wonder of Book I, and in later books grew to became the young teacher named Iris. You will hear me trying to define this transition ad nauseum to overcome my insecurity of not having explained it enough. Sorry, but not too sorry.

Iris is the girl who defined my late teens through mid-life. She was level-headed because she had to be. And surprise, surprise, the conscience nee alter-ego of my fascinating life is a manifestation named Cleve. I first thought Cleve was the masculine animus in me. Now I think this "other" gender of myself is my conscience speaking. Maybe Cleve is a chromosome imbalance, or does everyone have this mix?

Hmmm. Maybe we better not pull at this next thread?

I've asked The Writer to include only the good parts of my life in this script just like I did in the play. I don't know if it's fair, but I want to focus on the consequences of goodness. The Writer is my mature self, closest to the person I am now – I guess. She has a lot to say about a lot of things, especially about trees. She marvels at their durability; of course their slogan is, "Don't let your limbs fall off – keep em movin'." Trees have such a sense of humor.

Lights dim on the AUTHOR and. CLEVE steps into the spotlight. His voice is raspy and strong.

CLEVE

I've been discussed as though I'm as wise as an owl. Your conscience? Well, jobs are drying up so I'll live with whatever description you impose on me.

A simile is a comparison between two things using the words "like" or "as."

We virtuals are good guys. And God knows we've been brainwashed with the goodness inherent in stardust. There's stardust in all things, like us, and we know it has infused us with its power. It moved your thought process, dear author, to bring virtuals like me into reality. How else could I be talking to you? Controversial? Probably. But science has been on top of this for years.

Cleve remains one letter short of Clever.

All five books in the series defy time. I am the same character in the book as the guy who is talking to you right now. I'm in your head; scriptogenesis is happening, and you and I are closer than you think. When you read your novel or short story, where is it that you go? You go into the virtual world of fiction! That's my house and you are welcome.

Sorry, I'm getting a bit loud, but I get off on the fact that writing transforms thinking and possibly behavior too. Right now we are coming to you in real time from a virtual world which puts us smack dab in the middle of reality. I'm trying to prove that the book is as much history as it is fiction.

You can't read Alice In Wonderland and not go down the rabbit hole with her because you are seeing it in your mind's eye in real time. Your virtual-to-real-world headset is built in. So with just a few more tweaks, guys like me will soon move from VR, Virtual Reality ,to PR, Pure Reality.

You know what I say, hang on to your ticket stub. Whatever the Director wants to call this performance, he must admit it's history in the making!

He mockingly beats his chest.

I, Cleve, am predicting on this very opening night of *The Shelter of Trees* that virtuals are no longer second class characters. They are PR, Pure Reality, and they are here to stay. Okay, I'd better hightail it before they get the hook.

He starts toward the curtain and turns back around saying,

Mark my words. This is going to happen soon. So when I talk about virtual reality I'm not talking about stardust. Stardust is proven to be in our PR, Pure Reality. The power of stardust in us *is* the source of our goodness, that message just needs to seep in to the public's psyche a little deeper.

We are convinced that writers who connect with their stardust can lift their stories onto the Stardust String of Stories that travels through the universe. There they will remain forever, negating the old saying that nothing lasts.

Go ahead and draw what you think the Stardust String of Stories looks like, or draw yourself as an avatar trying to catch its tail. Symbols will do.

The trees begin to sway in unison, murmuring something about Cleve that we can't make out.

Another audience member stands up.

AUDIENCE MEMBER

It's heavy all right, Cleve, like a ton of bricks. We'll need a website to refer to for scientific proof. Now you want us to draw a picture?

CLEVE

I just want you to try out your creative wings, you know get your stardust juices flowing and try something new. Cleve whispers under his breath that there's a grumbler in every audience.

PEAR KNOWING TREE

Did you hear that? Cleve just said, "The Stardust String of Stories!" He knows about it.

MAPLE KNOWING TREE

Don't underestimate Cleve. We have always known about the Stardust String of Stories. We're so full of stardust stories our branches sag with them. Cleve probably got it from us since we tell stories over and over, even after they've made it up on the String where they are preserved for the next generation of saplings.

The sound of soft footsteps comes from the back of the stage. It's Myay, the really young one.

MYAY

Trees remind me of things that grow, and I'm glad I grew into Iris. I was the beginning of her career as a teacher and writer. Must have been my good business sense. I hope my business plan makes it up on the String. If it does, and I retire to The Story Hotel, I will live in literature forever, and with Cleve being so clever, we will never ever sever our ties, oh clever Cleve you are so wise….

CLEVE

Myay, put a lid on it my dear child, this isn't the book. We're trying to be serious here and give the audience something to chew on.

MYAY

Cleve, the stories of City Brick are destined to be classics, at least in our own minds. I would like my poem to be part of them – so for your listening pleasure.

Dramatically she recites her poem shown on page 22 of the book, entitled,

A Story's Crown Is Fleeting

A Stardust String of Stories
That travels up on high
Captures each new story
Like a spider traps a fly

Spiraling at the speed of light
The story keeps its Grip
While the string flaps its tail
In a Game of Crack the Whip

But a good story hold
Attaching to the string
And before the next one comes
For one instant it is king

AUTHOR

Sometimes it feels like Iris was doing the writing inside of her the whole time. Maybe there never was a Myay.

AUDIENCE MEMBER

Don't confuse us. I thought this play would clear things up. Do we have to write a poem now?

AUTHOR

It's not confusing if you believe in what miracles stardust can create in the realm of your imagination. You don't have to write a poem, or take any opportunity offered to you. This format is meant to be interactive. Here poetry happens, but I would be honored if you chose to write any stardust words in poetry or prose. They might just make it up to the String one day.

She winks at him.

Can we celebrate trees?

Please?

I believe

I believe

I believe

THE AUTHOR

Let's take a listen once again to what the trees have to say.

The trees respond with a literary tribute of their own, an excerpt from Robert Frost's 'Birches.' Page 25.

I'd like to go by climbing a birch tree,
And climb black branches up a snow-white trunk
Toward heaven, till the tree could bear no more,
But dipped its top and set me down again.
That would be good both going and coming back.
One could do worse than be a swinger of birches

Write down on your note pad what might be going on in Frost's mind as he wrote this poem.

Notes, Images, Creative Thoughts

____

____

____

____

____

____

____

____

____

____

____

____

BIRCH KNOWING TREE

Ah, love that Robert Frost, don't you all? We trees share not a blood type, but a stardust type. It makes our woody family quite extraordinarily bright.

The Writer enters and sees that the stagehands have added signs that hang from the trees saying," I'm not just majestic, I'm magic" and "I am Ancient and Rooted; I am a Stardust Carrier."

Another from the audience stands up.

AUDIENCE MEMBER

I get that this is historical fiction about the phases of your life, like typical phases in any human being. But you've added Cleve who has been there all along to keep your backbone strong; Cleve isn't a phase. And as to your stardust theory, I have read about stardust being ubiquitous, a big "u" word as Myay would say.

The audience chuckles over that.

I suppose you feel these phases should be included as a legitimate part of your memoir because Cleve and stardust are part of you. But I think that talking trees puts this memoir square in the fantasy genre. Something like that can only happen in fairy tales.

Genre is not a literary device. It is defined as a literary category like fiction, non-fiction, poetry, or drama.

AUTHOR

Bravo to you, and thank you so much for your attention. You came to interact with this script and you've been open to its creativity. You are right on about the narration and the increasing presence of stardust creeping into the plot as a metaphor.

I want to repeat that the easiest way to think about a *metaphor* is to think of a comparison without ever using the words "like" or "as." Let's use the title of Myay's poem on page 22 as an example, *A Story's Crown Is Fleeting*. Myay **does not say** that a story is **like** a crown, or a story is **as** fleeting as something else. She simply refers to a story having a crown. We know that stories don't have crowns, but she is being creative and pulling the two ideas together metaphorically.

We know too that stardust, which is tangible, is not really goodness because goodness is intangible. But we use literary tools to form a metaphor and pull stardust and goodness together. We call goodness "tenor" which means tone, or thing being described. We use the term "vehicle" for the object to describe goodness which is stardust. Try coming up with a metaphor of your own and you will remember it better for having created one.

Let's consider two genres. We'll compare the pure fantasy genre with historical fiction. Fantasy usually includes magic. My virtuals are unconventional, but they're not magical. Fantasy can also involve imaginary worlds. The City Brick series is set in the 1950's City of Jennings, a very real place. A strict fantasy trope, and we'll get into tropes later, usually involves a good vs. evil plot. Book I, *The Shelter of Trees,* is our focus and the plot is all about good not evil.

But there is a genre that offers a middle ground in which *The Shelter of Trees* can fall. It's called Historical Fantasy. This genre blends history and fantasy.

The Knowing Trees are perfect for this genre. In order to bring attention to their importance, and to do it creatively, I animated them and gave them stature.

Talking is how we convey important thoughts and feelings so I used the idea of talking trees to inform readers that trees have vital attributes. I thought I could best convey this if it came from the trees themselves. The Historical Fantasy genre gave me and them the chance to do that.

So in defense of the trees I can only say that since I was a child I have been drawn to trees by some unexplainable magnetism. Maybe because for many of my early years they were my only friends.

I was an avid reader, always dreaming of being in another place with exotic trees. They're part of the ecosystem that protects this planet. They are life-saving agents providing the oxygen we need to breathe. I choose to think of trees as partners because of their importance, their shade, and their kaleidoscope of color throughout the seasons.

Think about the importance of trees and write down your thoughts. We'll continue this discussion in Scene Two.

End of ACT I, Scene One

Notes, Images, Creative Thoughts

ACT I
Scene Two
Book Pages 39 - 69

AUTHOR

So in this unconventional play that our Director calls a presentation and I call a workshop, we'll exchange papers and learn from the ideas of others. After you've read it, add your best compliments in the margin and hand it back.

The audience exchanges papers and the DIRECTOR reluctantly gives them time to read them, to comment, and hand them back.

We were talking about trees that are critical to our survival. I didn't go out on a limb, pun intended, to bring the voices of trees to my memoir. I relished having the opportunity in this memoir to relay that trees are some of our best allies on this third rock from the sun, and I am grateful for them. But to understand that they could possibly have something to say about their standing here may require meditation in order to hear it.

The Oxford dictionary says that a pun is a way to exploit various meanings of words, to play with them essentially, have a little fun with them, When you hear it's a play on words, it's usually a pun that's being referred to.

The Author shrugged in a manner of I hope you accept that but if you don't it's okay.

Old as they are, the Major Oak and the Pine step to the front of the stage and speak together:

THE MAJOR OAK and METHUSELAH PINE

Yes, the thought of us trees was very dear to Myay, but we have dear friends across the globe who consider us dear to them also. You see our wooden trunks and branches are like vaults, keeping carbon dioxide locked away while we give off oxygen to provide air that is filtered and clean.

Our silent work is critical to the health and survival of this Earth. If it is ignored for too much longer we may not be around for the next generation, and that would be a calamity. Of course Myay saw us plenty in her other favorite book *Around The World In 1,000 Pictures*. With her we are quite famous.

The audience hears the chant, "Rah, Rah, Sis Boom Bah" coming from the direction of the rest of the Knowing Trees as the Author turns toward them and says,

AUTHOR

Oh c'mon now, we're talking about the '50s, but nobody says that anymore.

The sound of their leaves rustling could be heard again and has the audience wondering what the sound means in tree-speak.

There's a hush as the lights go down—momentarily. Cleve is seen walking through the trees as he looks up and says,

CLEVE

They really do talk, these trees do. They talk when they have something to say. Often it's about the weather, and sometimes they talk about us. They provide our world with what we need to exist and they are deadly proud of that. They don't talk about growing in phases; they talk about having nine lives. Freud must have over heard them.

CHINESE ELM

More than Freud hears us, Cleve. We started this Green Music Box of the World when our tropical brothers and sisters made themselves into a belt and turned the rainforest green. They're not in *The Shelter of Trees*, but I am. I'm featured on Page 51, and so what if I wasn't Chinese.

I was getting old during the 1950s and I didn't care what anyone said about me, because I understood the title of Book II. I can relate to *The Shelter of Cool Confidence.* I knew I was on my way out, but what good would it have been to give up and shed my leaves. I wanted to shade the Hansel and Gretel House just as long as Malone needed me to. And it was my pleasure.

The Writer hastily appears on stage, interrupting him rather enthusiastically.

THE WRITER

Thank you, Elm, you're such a great example of commitment and loyalty. And Cleve, the Freud thing? We virtuals are not holograms of alien avatars. Each of us is an important part of the Author. We are a Chorus, a collective noun, a stardust constellation of one person's thought. We are a script still being written.

Cleve puts his hands up signaling, "Okay already."

IRIS steps forward to intervene with The Writer and Cleve, and says in a calming voice,

IRIS

Lest we forget, Book I is about trees and stardust and us four virtuals, well Myay mostly. But this is Book VI.

She turns and points directly at the audience.

And now it's about all of you too. You are participants in this discussion. You are characters in this book-to-interactive-dialogue. We invite you to celebrate the light that shines in you by revealing your own stardust words. We made that clear in the book on Page 37.

AUTHOR

I've added elements to the *performance* that I hope enhances an understanding of the book. We begin with a heavy emphasis on the trees and we'll transition into new territory, new twists of the threads. You know, threads beyond the text. And your participation makes things more entertaining, sort of like we are in a nightclub skit and the entertainer makes things personal by including the audience.

It gives them a" kick." That's a '50's expression for awesome. So we evolve from book to skit if we choose. Pick your poison, instead of discussing we can certainly re-enact scenes.

AUDIENCE MEMBER

Well, I'd like to stick to our discussion. You've convinced me as to the importance and legacy of trees. They are underrated and probably underappreciated. I can accept also that the cast members are aspects of one being which is you, but you're here now simultaneously with them. How does that work? And I'll have to do a free-write to unload my thoughts about stardust.

CLEVE

Please, by all means do a free-write. And look, you make great points. I can't explain the four dimensional thing that goes on among us, except to say memory manifests itself in the author and up popped us. And the stardust thing took me a long time too. But hang on. You'll get it.

Notes, Images, Creative Thoughts

The Game of Clue

It was The Knowing Trees
In the City of Jennings
With The Mud.

CLEVE puts his hands up in a what-else-can-I-say, truth is stranger than fiction gesture, then begins a slow stroll through the trees and speaks again,

CLEVE

These trees, I swear, they know all the neighbor ladies who live on Helen Avenue. They know intimately the ones who adore Malone. She is the neighbor they depend on, the woman who became known as The Queen. You know, I bark a lot, but having a person like Malone to go to when there's trouble, well that's got to be the best kind of medicine. I wouldn't bark at that.

Cleve walked past the houses on Helen Avenue in Book I, and protected the names of the residents. But we can now say they were Betty, Marge, Evelyn, and Bessy. They were good and kind, a lot like Malone, special women who helped each other through thick and thin and were there for each other during hard times. He stops, and faces the audience.

So listen, it's a small town setting, but you really would like the neighbors and the trees and most everything else in Jennings. I hope before we end this thing that you'll like me a little bit too. I know I'm prickly so I ask for tolerance. Tolerance for my being… well, for my being Cleve.

CHINESE ELM

Hey folks, are you feeling it out there? The Author asked earlier if you are with her. If you're not yet, you will be. You just have to get to know us, or the idea of our partnership with you. Just like your wonderful neighbors, no matter where you live, we trees will sprinkle the environment with shade and beauty, and you won't find more loyal friends.

All we ask for is a little water and sunshine and we'll pop up at the roots and stay by you forever if we can. We're like the Stardust String of Stories that spirals forever and ever. Not much is permanent or even long lasting, but our longevity is a peaceful idea to hang on to when other ideas fizzle.

Another softly lit aura appears as the Author enters the stage and ponders her beautiful sister Sue who is pictured on page 60 of the book. She remembers Sue's deep compassion that seemed to make her more than human, more of guardian angel kind of being.

In her reverie, she smiles contemplating the goodness of Sue who suggested that Myay read Nancy Drew to help her understand things. That's what big sisters are for.

Cleve comes on stage and addresses the Author.

Cleve

Can I break up your séance and get in on this please? There's one thing Myay understood fully without any help from Nancy Drew or anybody else and that was Mud! Luckily, sister Sue came to the rescue when Myay would get a little too destructive with her slinging of mud balls. And Sue shared the kindness of the Malones, pitching in until the notice went up in the yard: *Warning, Goliath Lives Here.* Actually, behind the scenes, I'll tell you that Sue pitched in, in more ways than one. And she was sooo clever, much like me. I must say the Author's human family were pretty crafty. They gave us life. I'd say that's pretty clever.

The Writer re-appears.

THE WRITER

Cleve, let's not get into the weeds of who is human and who is virtual. It's not as important as what's being said. It's all in the books, and readers enjoyed the narration. It kept them guessing, but let's keep our focus on Myay's enchantment with mud and trees. They were central in her young life. And they are not trite subjects.

After all, there was stardust in the clay soil and it seeped into the mud surrounding the tree roots. Mud and trees were objects that sparked Myay's first impressions of the world around her. Those impressions turned out to be prophetic and they stuck.

The Knowing Trees needed soil and the soil was rich with stardust. They grew like Myay, in Goodness and Joy. The fact that we return to the stardust we find in clay mud carries a little weight, Cleve.

CLEVE

I guess so, "From stardust thou art and to stardust thou shalt return."

The Writer rolls her eyes at that and walks with the Author over to a bench under the trees.

THE AUTHOR

I think it will be best if we team up to keep our illustrious Cleve on track, and explain what's going on between the lines of this book. I don't want anyone getting the idea that the plot is skin deep. I know I was reluctant to disclose a sub-plot that wasn't all peaches and cream, but I'll say it again.

I didn't want *A Tree Grows In Brooklyn* tone to this memoir. The whole series should be a way to learn the joy of reading. I also set out to create a delightful way to appreciate the art of writing, and of goodness and humor, purely for its own sake. Now I have another opportunity in this format, whatever it is, to expose threads that I couldn't before. They are different and enlightening, and they run beneath the fabric of the text. Do you care if the Director is a little put out that we may run over our time?

THE WRITER

Not at all, I'm in. And I do agree. But it is a little baffling that you choose to do it now. I guess you wanted to paint an almost perfect picture in your memoir, and not call attention to anything that wasn't joyful and good? You've spoken through me, and I too want to clarify things in these pages that should be brought to light. I just don't always know what they are.

I guess your unpredictable nature is human, something I wouldn't know about. I do know we can't underestimate our audience or our readers. They're savvy to the fact that there's many nuances, metaphors, literary devices and a sub-plot that is implied in the book but not revealed. I want to enlighten and explain these things.

THE AUTHOR

Deal. I want to reveal most everything, but maybe not all the details of the hidden sub-plot which I've asked you to contain. I know there's a chance too that Iris, who thrives on uncovering what's hidden in stories like mine, could just open things up at any time. She has a mind of her own. For now, let's keep it quiet and a little bit muddy.

THE WRITER

Yep, it's about mud all right. Too frivolous to reflect on in a memoir? Too childish to take the time to write about? Too infantile to be literary? Well the subject is more of an interesting, scientific endeavor than is apparent in the text. Just because the dialogue is in large part from the perspective of a young person, I'm pretty sure adults can identify with it. I shouldn't have to say this, but take a look at a classic like *Oliver Twist.* It was read and enjoyed by young and old alike.

I would not be so presumptuous as to say *The Shelter of Trees* is a social critique as is said of *Oliver Twist*. However, there are similarities in that Mr. Brownlow was Oliver's benefactor and Ben Abel, the proprietor of the Drug Store, was Myay's. Ben Abel gave her wings - her first bike. He allowed her to read all the books, magazines and comics at his drug store. He even had her and her mother to dinner in his nice home.

Also consider *Harry Potter*, Scout and Jem of *To Kill A Mocking Bird* and of course there are others. Child protagonists appeal to the child in us. We never forget the days of our childhood when we are so full of wonder, basic psychology and fresh stardust.

Myay's fascination with mud was like any other object or toy put in front of a youngster, a diversion – until it became a springboard for much more. It was the first element she came in contact with that had to do with brick making. Ring a bell?

Of course, she didn't know it then, but stars align and realign throughout life and the mud led to clay that eventually led her down the Stardust Kingdom Trail which was covered in stardust words. Those words finally led her to the brick four-family flat in North St. Louis. What a journey; I need a breath.

Anyway it was mud that moved her up to a world above the trees, above the brick palace and into the Land of Goodness and Joy. No sub-plot interruptions here, just an upward trajectory.

CLEVE

I have to jump in or I won't get a word in edgewise with you two. This discussion leads to the next episode, From Mud Balls To Mud Masks. By this point on Page 62, we are feeling the intense desire of a young girl who is ready to break out of her first home like she broke out of her buggy. She feels like *Wonder Woman*, ready to take on the neighborhood with her mother at the helm of course. Mud has a basic set of chemicals, but a mud mask moves the elements into a much more complex mixture.

Isn't it reasonable to begin to see the stardust connection at this point. You know Sherlock Holmes could just as easily have said, "Elemental my dear Watson, Elemental" and the outcome would have been the same. Anyway, this episode puts us back on that springboard to find out that dirty feet stuck in the mud can lead to beautiful faces covered in mud, that all things we encounter growing up really are relative in a yin yang sort of way.

The Director walks on stage.

DIRECTOR

The script is making me think--hard. Speaking of a yin yang way, in Myay's own way she considers herself a pretty astute business woman. What kid thinks about a business plan anyway? She had to be more Iris than Myay all along. Anyway, let's turn our attention to something we think the audience is clamoring for, a much needed Q&A session.

Huh?

Q&A Session

DIRECTOR

Okay CUT

AUDIENCE MEMBER

Cut what? This is live.

DIRECTOR

The Author wants your participation and I have agreed, so we cut the action to give you a chance to ask your questions before we proceed. Make sense?

The audience claps, and one by one they stand and speak. Evidently they have been listening closely. But this is eerily similar to what happened in the Author's Book entitled, A Gathering of Stardust, whereby several folks stood and asked questions.

FIRST AUDIENCE QUESTION

If you wanted to be mysterious about the sub-plot, you definitely have our attention. But my question is less shadowy and more practical. Why do the virtuals think they need to encourage us to write?

SECOND AUDIENCE QUESTION

Your team approach will help us unravel more threads so it should lead to better understanding. But tell me, how did the Knowing Trees get so smart?

THIRD AUDIENCE QUESTION

I just want to know, since you say this story isn't just kid's stuff, is the idea of stardust something like a cyber protein?

FOURTH AUDIENCE QUESTION

Thanks for this session, because if you don't want us to consider the series as simply fantasy, but a somewhat historical account of real life, can you prove that anyone has seen the Stardust String of Stories?

CLEVE

Cleve holds his hands up in a gesture that signals he wants the audience to break off their questions.

All right, you are all starting to sound like the Doubting Thomas that I am. I see you are going to have lots of questions. The Writer and the Author will be happy to answer them. But I've been told to keep the story of Myay and Iris on track.

A grumbling of consent is heard in the audience and the Author steps out front.

THE AUTHOR

Well I'm proud this group is generating such good questions. If our cast can't come up with good answers then we shouldn't have written this Companion book. The Iris in me knows from teaching brilliant students that your own observations may well be the most creative. But here's a go at answering your questions. And we *will* stay on track, Cleve.

She said this with a wink and a smile.

Let's begin with the first question about why we virtuals encourage writing. Remember, our passion is to be your Writing Companions, every one of us.

The stagehands bring out two chairs for The Writer and the Author to sit in.

THE AUTHOR

Ah, how kind of you. Bringing us these chairs is significant to the purpose of the whole series. Helpfulness is in some ways an old-fashioned trait, but one that leads us to becoming The Land of Goodness and Joy. Random acts of kindness add up like a stack of bricks ready to host the Disadvantaged Royalty who are as well-hidden in the series as the sub-plot of *The Shelter of Trees.*

THE WRITER

Answer to question About writing. Yes we want to encourage you to write.

The process of creative writing is like smelting and brick making. And the comparison is not a stretch. During smelting, metals are extracted from ore. During writing kernels of good ideas are extracted from written drafts.

A brick is the product of an industrial process that is multi-faceted. One must examine the earth's soil to find a suitable clay, then process raw materials through a development phase of mixing ingredients to effect change, then heating and cooling them. Sounds like when a teenager's hormones are raging to get to a new stage of development. It's like what Myay went through to become Iris. It's also a lot like raw ideas spewing out of the furnace of your mind, then being refined to become final essays or stories.

The brick making ingredients are clay, sand, water, lime and other additives. The ingredients of a written piece are facts from research, ideas, and imaginative thought. Natural elements coalesce into brick, conceptual elements into writing, and Myay into Iris. If you are writing and someone says you are industrious, they are right on.

I remind you that our premise is that all things contain stardust, and the three processes I just mentioned are in part fueled by stardust. But one of these processes is kind of magical. Stick with me.

Brick are fashioned with the intention of creating a sustainable end product. Words are fashioned with the intention of entertaining, educating or to make progress by cutting through the red tape of ignorance into new understandings. A character like Myay, written into the annals of literature, is fashioned with the intention of becoming a young adult.

Some characters are created with a deeper purpose, to change the world. All these processes are intentional. The brick-maker intends to provide shelter, The Writer to promote understanding, the character to grow and change. In our case, the character seems to have more than one intention because she is part of a very human author.

So maybe she does want to change the world. Intention is a defining factor for a writer. The first character I created was The Little Maestro. I intended for him to change the fate of the rainforest by harmonizing its discordant music – and he did. I intended to raise awareness not just entertain.

My intention came from my passion to have a character make a difference and set an example. A writer who understands that words are made of stardust like everything else naturally has good intentions and will have good outcomes.

Think about what characters you've come to know in literature. Which ones exist for the sake of the story and which ones exist to make the world a better place. They're both essential and depend on the intention of The Writer.

Notes, Images, Creative Thoughts

Getting to the Magic

In what we call the real world you can't go backwards in time. But when you write, you can re-create what happened in time by pulling events through the view finder of history into the vista of today. That my dear friends is an evolutionary process that only writing can bring about. Time does not exist inside the stardust words of a writer. The words defy the constraint of time by accessing memory.

As a writer, I can create a rainforest that has been saved by The Little Maestro, not ruined by deforestation. I can, therefore, show the world the way forward into a future of furtive plants and trees just by writing it into existence. Writing with the intention of using good stardust words and ideas is how we bring an intellectual evolution to our reality.

The audience seems to respond as they make use of their notepads.

That was a long answer but an extremely important one. I'm sure The Author will be less wordy as she answers the next question.

THE AUTHOR

Answer to question about the Knowing Trees. They were communicating through their roots when we were writing on cave walls.

Well, it goes back to the intention of why a writer like me created the Knowing Trees in the first place. It wasn't just to give Myay something to look at. They had specific functions that needed to be brought to the attention of 21st Century readers. When I wrote *The Little Maestro*, Iris was in another role, the main writer at the time, logging hours of extensive research about the flora and fauna of the rainforest to be able to create a character to save it. The rainforest has a long and mystical history. The rainforest was once a lush and exceptional part of the natural world.

As civilization progressed, it was apparent that in order to exist, people had to enter into partnership with the trees because they provided life sustaining oxygen. Some creator, mighty wise, knew that the planet needed oxygen, thus there were trees. They loomed large in the rainforest belt and provided not only oxygen, but shade from the sun, beauty in hues of green, and shelter from their wood.

Iris took this tree research as far as the scholarly information would go. But it turned out the message and goodwill of my character, The Little Maestro, didn't help. The trees have been continually felled and the rainforest decreased. And too, some of the trees wanted to keep their history secret. They weren't ready to reveal their ways of communicating through their roots. Their speech has a lot to do with vibration as the roots travel underground. Trees were obviously made to be smart, and it was because of the good intention of their creator. Now they're speaking up again in this book, trying again, to make people realize their relevance. And they are using their own paper bi-products to do it in the very pages of this book.

THE WRITER

Answer to the question about stardust. It certainly could be proven to have the power of a protein.

As to what stardust is, well it's as Myay says, a combination of CHNOPS: Carbon, Hydrogen, Nitrogen, Oxygen, Phosphorous and Sulphur. And you might be correct. I wouldn't doubt at all that the stardust recipe may one day be seen to be as important as a vital protein is for staying alive.

You have to admit, the stars have the corner on longevity. Stardust as a source of goodness is associated with light without which we probably wouldn't survive. It's mysterious and I suppose its miniscule inclusion in all things that makes a body wonder why it's there if not for a spectacularly good reason.

THE AUTHOR

Answer to the question about the Stardust String of Stories. Of course it's real.

Okay let's move on to the question about the Stardust String of Stories. Is your deceased grandmother who you never met but only heard about real? You've never seen her, but Iris claims she's seen The Stardust String of Stories. She says it exists not just in outer space but in thc space of the mind.

She recounts that when one of her students does well on a written story, it's like his/her self-image takes off like a rocket. This is why we encourage students. It makes a difference in their performance and their confidence does skyrocket.

The once struggling young student writing a story is now part of something bigger, something that put his or her hope on the tail of a kite and sent it flying high. Personal success leads to a student's ego inflating enough to want to perform even more with renewed hope to do even better in the future. That story of how a teacher creates self-confident students has become timeless.

It is now part of a story data base of literary accomplishments that a creative writer like Iris calls the Stardust String of Stories. And yes, it spirals through the stars where the first story was born. The stardust words in stories seek their home among the stars. It's simple string theory.

Again she winks.

The Author asks the stage hands for assistance in handing out a few more note cards to the audience to be used later.

CLEVE steps forward once more, smiling. He has a microphone, a two-way radio, and an iPhone. He swings a lantern like an altar boy swings an incense burner as he calls the audience to attention.

CLEVE

Hear ye, hear ye, to all participants of City Brick, whether you're in the audience, classrooms, auditoriums, group gatherings, or book club meetings, we want to spark the stardust in you. Seek it in yourself, and your thoughts will be harmonious and balanced, filled with the heady excitement of pursuing the next idea that makes what you write truly new and creative ideas. We all hope you have lots of fun in the process.

Till PART II, It's Just me Cleve,

On Letter Short of Clever

AUTHOR

Write out your thoughts about the answers we provided. It's another chance to interact. And maybe, based on what you write, it could be the beginning of another story, your story, on the Stardust String.

Lights fade slowly to black.

End of ACT I, Scene Two

Notes, Images, Creative Thoughts

ACT II
Scene One
Book Pages 70 - 122

As the lights come up for Scene Two there are now new signs up in the tree tops. The Maple looms largest among the trees as the Author reflects on Myay's love for them.

AUTHOR

Growing up, my world was small. Things in my environment meant a lot to me, like the Maple outside the kitchen window and the Chinese Elm in the postage stamp front yard of our Hansel and Gretel House. Reading about trees in any poems or prose that came my way was a thrill.

I can see why Myay offers a quote from Mary E. Wilkins Freeman regarding the Elm, and I'll provide a little something from Robert Frost regarding the Maple tree. In all honesty I'm not sure if Myay was a little literary savant, a sassy showoff, or maybe a bit of both.

Along with these awesome quotes, we have not given enough attention to the "Important Quotes" that run through the episodes, so here's what Myay would say about them:

Take Note
There is an important Quote
On many a page
    They should not be underrated
    And so it should be stated
    They're from a mysterious sage
The sage is a kid like me
Who offers them for free
Without a living wage
    Yet I promise to pursue
    Words of inspiration for you
    I vow it upon this very stage

And so Myay's quote by Mary E. Wilkins Freeman appeared in the pages of scene one, but it is meant to be combined with Robert Frost's poem - for emphasis. We'll start with Ms. Wilkins' tribute to the Elm tree:

> "It became at such time, to some minds, something akin to a testimony of God. Something there was about the superb acres of those great branches curving skyward and earthward with matchless symmetry of line which seemed to furnish an upward lift for thought and imagination."

The Author reflects that Myay has always been older than her years to have referred to such a heady quote by Ms. Wilkins. She adds a poem by Robert Frost and asks the audience to listen closely.

Evening In A Sugar Orchard

From where I lingered in a lull in March
outside the sugar-house one night for choice,
I called the fireman with a careful voice
And bade him leave the pan and stoke the arch:
'O fireman, give the fire another stoke,
And send more sparks up chimney with the smoke.'
I thought a few might tangle, as they did,
Among bare maple boughs, and in the rare
Hill atmosphere not cease to glow,
And so be added to the moon up there.

The moon, though slight, was moon enough to show
On every tree a bucket with a lid,
And on black ground a bear-skin rug of snow.
The sparks made no attempt to be the moon.
They were content to figure in the trees
As Leo, Orion, and the Pleiades.
And that was what the boughs were full of soon.

Does any line in the Wilkins Freeman tribute or the Robert Frost poem speak to you? Responding to poetry is responding to stardust words that shape the course of the world.

Notes, Images, Creative Thoughts

THE WRITER

She gazes at Myay, who is still on stage, as if remembering the love of poetry she had in her youth, and her love of reading. She laughs about never being a frilly little girl but wearing overalls mostly and flinging mud balls with aggression.

AUTHOR

Can one so young be aggressive? It feels like an odd word to describe…me?

THE WRITER

Don't confuse me with you. I am a proud virtual, and I try to front for you when you are too afraid to speak for yourself. But I'm only one part of you. So it's natural to have cracks in our thinking, yours and mine. It's not surprising that you might say energetic and I say aggressive. Thoughts can often run counter.

AUTHOR

You think I'm too afraid to speak for myself?

THE WRITER

Maybe I overstated by using that adjective, but this performance is a companion to your memoir. And it's a challenge to make sure we've included all that is needed for a reader to not only "re-view" but to understand the dynamics of the narration. Here's a News Flash: it's groundbreaking, not just because a book is being elaborated on in a different format, but because the number of voices who are narrating it are sovereign and defy time. We virtuals have made a mark.

Each book was written in the recent past by us virtuals, but Myay's part comes from the distant past, mid-20th Century. What's more, since it has been written down, it will last long into the future. Yet here we are, on this outdoor stage under the stars, in the present moment.

I'm not sure how you did it, but you've uprooted parts of your life that are rooted in the past, and through your written memories those parts have manifested as us. I am one of your virtual characters who speak in a tense that is not only present, but immediate due to the effect it has on listeners and readers. I'm a virtual, but like Cleve I want to carve out my own destiny.

Like many of your previous characters, Myay has famously broken through the pages of memory to gain her place in the future of 21st Century literature. She must grab for the tail of the Stardust String of Stories, or she may never eternalize her stardust words. Cleve, Iris, and me, we have the same desire. Of course, nooo pressure at all on this.

AUTHOR

Thanks for always trying to help me "realize" what's true. I would say reaching the tail of that String is a high bar, especially for a virtual character, and Myay is still trying. But once stardust words are written, even in dialogue, the author's seat is secured in a literary time machine.

It's like a seat on The Enlightenment that took readers for an incredible flight in Book III. As a writer myself, I'll never stop grabbing for the tail in hopes to spin my body of work into a future perfect tense.

Future perfect tense is a wonderful tense that uses the words "*will have*" or "*shall have*."

Sometime in the future there will be a moment when The City Brick Memoir Series will have received rave reviews all cross the country. I'm sure you and I dear Writer have no disagreement on the fact that it *will* happen. With teamwork we will all see that day.

THE WRITER

No disagreement here. Like Myay I know when to tone down my rhetoric. I don't want a "Lady Jane" moment – not now or in the future perfect

They both laugh as an aura of a woman appears in the background, possibly Malone. The Writer remembers a saying of the Author's mother back in the day when they called her Malone, "where there's a will there's a way." Malone was taking a risk at her age to begin a career as a saleslady, and another risk having Myay along to sell cosmetics on neighborhood streets. Although kind and gentle, Malone was tough when she needed to be. She was always positive and could find ways to cope with the wavy boards of the Hansel and Gretel house. The Writer looks at the silhouette in the aura and speaks to the Author.

THE WRITER

You didn't appear in any of the books in the City Brick series, but you are now a member of the cast. I think Malone is with us too. She just doesn't have a speaking part. She is here because everything we do is connected to her heart.

She was our rock, and the days with her were precious. When I hear the words, these precious days, just like the song and the title of Anne Patchett's book, they go right through me.

The days that we have family around are when we are happiest, no tears, no sadness, just precious days. In those days, as Malone was preparing to start selling make-up, she explained the contents in her sample case to Myay and it was a rite of passage.

The idea of a rite of passage is one of those foreshadowing events that you choose not to explain, but one day you might think differently.

Rite of Passage is a literary technique that highlights a certain moment in a character's growth and development.

The Writer thinks about Myay who right now anxiously awaits another passage, a prompt that signals her back on stage to tell the audience of her heroic flight into her own future perfect tense.

Past Tense
Present Tense
Future Tense
Future Perfect Tense

The Director is Tense

The stagehands brighten the light over Myay. She looks eager to relate a once-in-a lifetime adventure that happened to her. A kidnapping? Or was she subconsciously determined to get beyond her Hansel and Gretel House postage stamp lawn, wavy boards, pre-teen longings and just rise above it all? Possibly, but who would have thought she would find herself among the friendliest aliens outside the planet. Or were they something other?

Our most unpredictable Maya steps closer to the spotlight and before telling her extraordinary story surprisingly takes a moment to enlighten her audience about the technology of Maple Trees. She says that their spinners are the original drones. This high tech conversation was a segue into her own tale about a flight to the firmament. A space odyssey indeed!

But just as Myay is set to begin, the Director makes an uncustomary appearance on stage. He is sweating and a little breathless.

DIRECTOR

I beg your pardon for this interruption, but I really need to inform everyone that we might go past midnight if we don't cut short our performance. Have mercy. You've been given a taste of how Myay can "carry on." So because you've read the book, and to keep the dialogue moving, I can only bring you excerpts from her account of the abduction.

He looks at the Author and says,

I guess it was an abduction. Right?

AUTHOR

She looks a bit skeptical, does not answer, and points toward Myay to begin her story. At once the audience starts to write in their notepads .Apparently the Director's question conjured up their own questions of what really did happen to Myay.

Myay

I know everyone thinks I'm a chatterbox, a chinwagger of a "c" word, so I'll obey our Director and just give you the highlights of this mysterious episode. The gist is that a kid goes airborne and doesn't even understand how or why. So, how's that for breaking news?

After rising up on foam steps of a bus, I was in a state of cerebral incoherence that I can't even explain. I was obviously experiencing a degree of trepidation over where I might be heading, but oddly enough I really wasn't afraid. In some ways I was piloting the flight.

Medically speaking, however, I believe I could have been in a fluorescent stupor. You may think I was dreaming, but I truly had to be awake for this extrasensory experience. How else could I have remembered such notable details like asking if I could visit the factory where they make halos, and noticing that angels look a lot like fireflies. Oh, Yessiree, those angels were fun and smart as whips too. But do not base my credibility on the incident, for I too am skeptical of its authenticity. I'm no naïve kid anymore.

Surely, you find this a flight of fancy, but I say it was a bolt out of the blue, because *something* billowed me off the bus, a bedazzling barrage of "b" words. Sorry, not sorry, and I'd love to expound about this but I'd better yield to the Director. I am a team player, so I'll skip to the end of an affair that I personally did not want to see end.

Thus, tragically, like pop goes the weasel, I popped out of my fluorescent stupor. The upside is that during my flight upward bound, or during a possible sleep apnea episode, I didn't need to catch a falling star. Wait for it: the trip qualified me as a bonafide Star Girl. Hey, it's the age of miracles. And you may hear later that my flight was something else entirely. Do stay tuned, and let the story *play* out. Get it?

AUTHOR

Star Girl, by the way, was the first book Myay remembered reading and the character of Star Girl was brewing inside her ever since, maybe the better word is fermenting. Believing in the truth of *Star Girl* being real is what led her to thoughts of what else was real and what was not.

In her mind truth had something to do with what God wanted to be real, because God told the truth. And God's truth came straight to her like a laser beam, penetrating the roof of her gymnasium-turned- church, St. Louise De Marillac, named for a woman who cared for the poor. Had the term Disadvantaged Royalty been coined during her lifetime, she would have sought them out and made sure they all had warm sweaters. She was not a virtual character of literature, but a real human hero whose passport is cleared for the Land of Goodness and Joy. I'm sure she's in residence there – but I digress. Excusez-moi!

Anyway, the church *was* a repurposed gymnasium and it *was* bit sparse. Oh but it did have an interesting Oak Tree that stood between the church and the school. Fascinated with trees, Myay couldn't hold herself back from remarking on the versatility of its acorns and partaking in their usefulness . Their uses were countless and could cure the worst case of boredom. I'll let your imagination run wild on this.

Notes, Images, Creative Thoughts

Trees sense changes, and the signs on the trees begin to flip forward, sort of bowing as they sway. This arboreal display is out of respect for Iris who is taking the stage. They love her because she researched their history and often calls them by their scientific names. At this point in the book's pages Iris entertains with An Ode To The Seasons Of The Dogwood and a story about the history of the Major Oak. She is a true literary archeologist and arborist to boot.

Iris would very much like to read them to you but fears for the mental health of the Director, so she refers the audience to pages 89 and 91 to enjoy a poetic revival of her research. After her short but stimulating interval the lights focus once again on Cleve who continues his narration of the walking tour of Jennings.

The Director looks pleased as he wipes his brow, but he is wary of the audience's curiosity as they continue to write about Myay's so-called abduction.

CLEVE

You'll note that Myay's house was a Hansel and Gretel type abode, a bit small but adequate. I should mention the somewhat tiny kitchen where Myay wrote a poem with her mother as they sat at the kitchen table that had the wobbly leg. Seemingly this creative session was the beginning of an avocation that has existed throughout her many phases, one of which is me. Her quest to perfect this literary gambit began at that very moment! And it's all thanks to Malone.

THE WRITER

Although the Hansel and Gretel house was built on love, there were moments of frustration for Myay. When she pestered her mother because she couldn't go with her sister, she was told to play with the dog. This didn't set well with Myay who despised the pooch, and thus swept her mother's guidance under the proverbial rug. It highlights a rare defiance, but she found a way out of things that frustrated her by spending her time thinking about her teachers, her beloved Daughters of Charity, their sweetness, beautiful faces and brilliant minds.

Cleve walks over to Myay and puts his arm around her.

CLEVE

You all can tell by now that our Myay is a bit impulsive, but such a good kid. She is, as you also know by now, an unpredictable *Star Girl.*

The Writer is pleased with the support Cleve gives Myay, and chuckles as she watches Myay pop back on stage and recite the first poem she ever wrote entitled, Lace Over The Moon. The message in the poem's last line is another example of what we call foreshadowing, yet we never really get to hear the details of what is being foreshadowed. Pity. Or maybe not.

The Writer decides to move on and rolls a portable spot light over to the Pear Knowing Tree to recite a passage from St. Augustine and set the stage for a scene of petition and forgiveness by Myay. Forgiveness for what? Well, forgiveness about a venial sin verses a little innocent tomfoolery. It's a big white snowball of a question that most kids have to answer at some time or other.

Myay, still standing with Cleve like a little angel kneels down on one knee with arms out toward the audience in a pleading gesture saying with her most dramatic voice,

Voice is a literary device and technique that illustrates how a writer choses words and sets a tone that defines a personal style that can be formal, humorous, or serious.

Myay

Now maybe I wasn't always an angel, but I can tell you I never wanted to let the nuns down. Yet one fateful day it was all ruined. I had to fess up, so I decided to confess a tiny transgression of a sin I had committed. I had hoped it was a venial sin, but it turns out that it was larceny. Being caught red-handed with white petals as evidence I was forced into a full confession.

I had made a small deposit of flower petals in the back of church, and was surreptitiously caught flat footed by the janitor. After this trickery and humongous humiliation, two horrible "h" words, I knew the rest of my life should be spent as Sister Agnes said, in sack cloth and ashes.

My beloved nun, however, could not break my spirit for I had the tenacity of Nancy Drew and the moxie of St. Theresa, my mother's patron saint, for there was no patron saint of sinners that I knew of.

Since I have the floor, and I hate to give it up but I have to, I will depart ACT II, Scene One on a high note by telling you I was forgiven by the powers that be, and there were many. 😊

Another "What's Cookin" Opportunity Awaits You.

ACT II
Scene Two

The Author told us previously that Iris, a woman of integrity, may no longer settle for secret sub-plots and foreshadowing devices that never come in to the light. And she seems to be getting more vocal and straightforward in her commentary.

Right here in Scene Two her assertiveness is turning the tables on the audience . Where will it wind up? Like the Chinese Elm, she must have read Book II, The Shelter of Cool Confidence!

DIRECTOR

At this point, the cast will entertain any questions or comments that any of you in the audience may have. You can enjoy the time to relax or to write your questions and ideas in the note pages we provided.

He exits the stage and a gentleman in the audience stands up.

AUDIENCE MEMBER

What are we really doing here? This format does offer a novel way to transition from the literary genre of a book to that of a play. I guess it's mostly narration to dialogue – sort of. But groundbreaking? Maybe or maybe not. I don't think any one of us in this audience is naïve enough to believe that a story about a kid with a psychological powerhouse of an imagination will explode norms of literary history or change a reader's perception - of anything! And personally, aside from the overall literary perspective, I doubt that your elusive stardust is the influencing factor that makes someone become a better person.

AUTHOR

"Readers' Theater" is the conversion of a literary work into a script for a performance.

Neither me nor any of the characters are writing to convince anyone that this page- to- stage dramatization is groundbreaking. I will say, though, that part of me, that part being The Writer, says it is because of the unique uses of personification of inanimate objects and chronogenesis, the manipulation of time. We're not out to prove that using them is revolutionary, but we have used them creatively and innovatively.

Personification is a literary device that gives human traits and characteristics to inanimate objects.

As to your not believing in stardust as a catalyst of goodness. Of course you doubt it. You are still seeking the stardust in yourself. But have an open mind. I use stardust somewhat metaphorically as the stimulus that powers the inherent goodness in people, motivating them toward good and away from evil.

Stardust is a trope upon which the whole City Brick Series is built. The goodness in a person's heart and mind is there because of the infusion of stardust in us. The reason I wrote a five-book memoir, and this challenging dramatic adaptation, is because I knew goodness up close and personal in the form of Malone. The world always needs a refueling of it to overcome evil.

If we are not engaged in creating the Land of Goodness and Joy, the land that we know will become a desert of inhumanity. A writer can only try to change his or her corner of the world so that the desert heat doesn't overwhelm.

AUDIENCE MEMBER

Well, with the many foreshadowing techniques that you've left hanging, I won't hold my breath waiting for you to reveal exactly how you've tried to create your corner.

AUTHOR

Let me try to make up for the mysteries I've left you with. The story of Book I, or the plot if you want to call it that, is not about anything as narrow or shallow as the whims and fancies of a little kid working through her maturation process. It's much deeper than that if you go beyond the text into what might be the purpose of writing about this in the first place.

It's about the extraordinary way Myay was influenced to become a person who cared about goodness. It's about the factors in her life that led her to seek the Land of Goodness and Joy. Revelatory enough?

In the case of Myay and Iris, they did it the only way they knew how to, through the use of words, stardust words that only spread light and love. Importantly, it's about the characters in her life who contributed to her becoming a "Malone Wannabe." Let's look at a few virtual characters in literature that led us to believe in the struggle to be good and make it up to the Stardust String of Stories:

Joe March of *Little Women* opened a school later in life whereas Myay and Iris became teachers. *Rebecca of Sunnybrook Farm* used her own inheritance to become a teacher and help her family in the meantime. How about *Pollyanna* who was always trying to bring happiness to those she met.

Isn't this what Myay and Iris are trying to do in their quest to let people know the satisfaction that comes from being enlightened and able to perform at their best. I can also cite *Anne of Green Gables* who sought goodness in the world around her, whereas Myay left no room for anything else but that.

Finally, I call your attention to Francie of *A Tree Grows In Brooklyn,* because she was some kind of influence on Myay from her early reading of classic books. Francie had her difficulties for sure; the times alone were hard, but she found a way out through books. Conversely, Myay actually found a way up.

Myay built her thoughts, words and deeds, in part, on the goodness she found in her family and in literature. Her stardust words were born in classic stories written by females. But since then many male protagonists have set good examples like Harry Potter, Luke Skywalker, Huck Finn, and Evan Matutinus, my Little Maestro who was born to save the rainforest.

I do hope these examples help you see through the text to its deeper meanings. These threads beyond the stardust words of the text are full of significance for people of all ages. This reformatting may not be groundbreaking but it is pioneering, and maybe cloud-busting as it makes its way toward the Stardust String of Stories.

Two of the Knowing Trees graciously step apart and let Iris enter the stage.

AUDIENCE MEMBER

Some of us out here think there's more going on than meets the eye. None of us thought it was just about the antics of a young girl. We knew there was lots to be learned in between the lines of each episode. So here for starters, how about the foreshadowing that relates directly to the sub-plot that you have directed The

Writer will not talk about it . We're on to that secret and it seems to be a big one. What's that about?

There's the episode about Myay being taken to heaven, or the hinterlands, with no explanation for it? Isn't that some kind of "unreliable narration" on your part? You had Myay saying that she just didn't know what was happening to her, but you also intimated that she was piloting the flight. Which is it, simply a child's dream, or a willful attempt to run away from something?

IRIS

We are not unreliable narrators, and we wouldn't try to trick you. We are trying to give you something that doesn't just slide down your throat like simplistic pablum, but something, as Cleve would say, to chew on. It does look like we've accomplished that because your passion is building as we proceed and we're not even finished.

The other thing we are doing is pushing the edges of creative writing beyond the black and white box it's in. We are using threads of many colors. Creative writing is a kaleidoscope that changes the outer edges of meaning to fit in other ways. It's a catalyst that makes *you* think out of the black and white box and into a phantasmagoria of colorful ideas, images and a bubbling cauldron of concepts.

If everything is laid out for you, as though the small pieces of colored glass in the kaleidoscope have vitrified into clear easily seen through glass. Then what does your mind have to do? It will freeze from boredom because there's no reason to inquire anymore; every detail and every nuance of the story has been handed to you. So why not just stop reading?

Well, the more you read for answers to mysteries in the plot, the more engaged you become. Stardust words of a text should keep you suspended outside the box. And it seems like that's where you are at. And I think that's great!

AUDIENCE MEMBER

So are you saying that readers have to be investigators? I don't want to work when I read; I want to enjoy. Like you said about the setting. I want the descriptions in a story to take me away – without effort.

IRIS

We all have different expectations from a story that we read. It sounds like one of yours is relaxation or pure entertainment. Me, I like an adventure. I want to be so engrossed that I'm part of the action even if it keeps me on the edge of my seat. But let me say that this discussion is coming very close to the kind of literary adventure that I find most fascinating, which is seeking the stardust in a story that leads to its hidden themes.

A good story always seems to reveal hidden subplots full of untapped ideas and exciting motifs. The story of Myay and Iris is a good story and it's not over yet.

So, let's talk about some of the elements of a good story and how they present themselves. In other words, let's get bookish.

Take Setting. There's nothing more peaceful than settling down with a book that pulls you into its setting right off the bat. This is another way that literature offers time travel. For moments you are suspended in a new place trying to grasp on to the delicious details of where the story is taking you.

I love the first moments in *The Shelter of Trees*. The setting is the sleepy little City of Jennings. But I was startled when I first met up with the Knowing Trees. Yes I met them like you did. Just because I was instrumental in creating them doesn't mean they didn't surprise me, and continue to surprise me. I bet many parents are surprised by their own children when they say or do certain things. The theory of relativity lives in the pages of fiction.

I actually think it festers there because fiction is like a quantum computer that cross references at light speed and merges reality with fantasy and of course possibility. If you haven't figured out that there's more to writing and reading fiction than any science textbook can offer. then you may understand the plot but not the story implications.

No disrespect, but I would ask you to stay open to the instant before discovery. The seconds before a new kind of knowledge enters your mind is the most exciting time there is. Writing fiction offers so many of those moments, just before the next word is written or the next thought forms. The moments before the birth of a new idea that never was before are the most adventure-filled and intellectually explosive moments you will ever have.

So should you be an investigator? For sure. But the idea of reading being some kind of work, well if that's your perspective, you and I are reading differently. I read because I want to be stunned by a set of stardust words that I've never seen put together before. Their novel arrangement can astonish me like nothing else, because they convey a new idea I never thought about before.

Reading fills me with new ideas and so I'm never empty. It's a whole different way of thinking about time spent inside a book. For me it's never work. It's wonder!

My best wishes for you to find what is the name of another of Ann Patchett's books, that *State of Wonder*.

Iris sits in a chair brought out by the stagehands.

It's the Catbird Seat.

Iris ponders. She has a somewhat sly smirk on her face which is unusual for her. A change in tempo must be coming.

IRIS

Setting: Let's change course right here mid-stream, and I'll ask you some questions. Get your notepads ready and tell me your thoughts about the signs that the trees hold. Should there be more props or is this rather sparse setting adequate?

Conflict: And what about some other key elements of the story starting with struggles and problem personalities and the like. Is it essential to the enjoyment of every plot?

____

____

____

____

____

Rising Action: What do you sense as the rising action in the book's portrayal of a young girl experiencing first sensations in the world as she grows up? Would you say they are believable based on your own life experiences?

____

____

____

____

____

Tone: Do each of the narrators feel the same about this little protagonist? Does Cleve sound convincing when he talks about Myay, the same as when he talks to Myay. If there is a difference in his tone, does it mean you are not understanding the ambiguity in Cleve?

____

____

____

____

____

Characters' Evolution: Do you feel any of the characters changing or growing intellectually in any of the scenes? Story-telling supposedly requires protagonists to follow a character arc so that you, the reader, can better connect with them emotionally. Does this exist in *The Shelter of Trees*, and if not is it a flaw in the story?

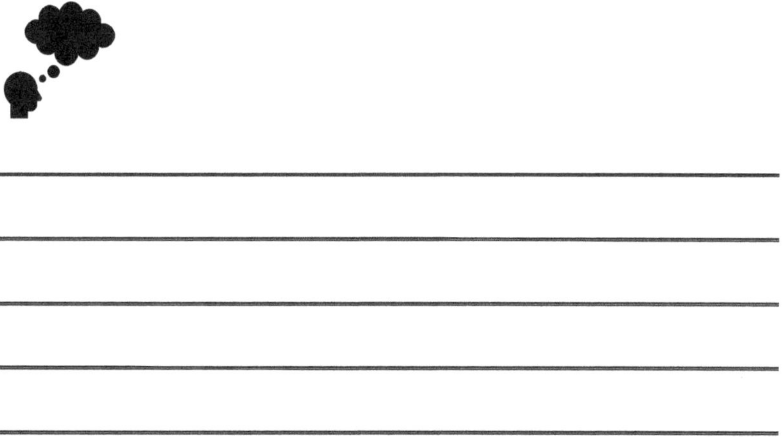

Themes: Would you agree that the broad theme of family values is part of the feeling among the characters? Is there any kind of sinister theme running through the plot? If so, explain who and what is involved.

Author's Style: This will be hard to describe, but give it a shot. We haven't discussed the diction of the characters which boils down to the author's choice of words. And we haven't discussed syntax, which is the way the words are put together to form sentences. Does either the diction or syntax have an effect on your reading experience in *The Shelter of Trees*?

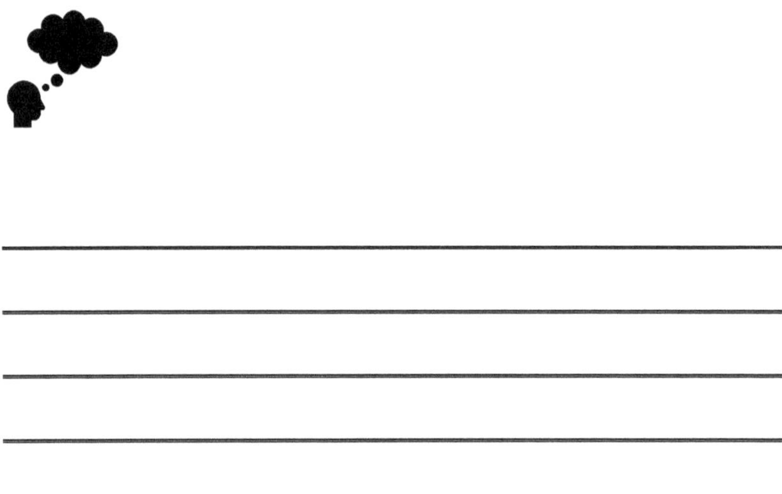

Dialogue: Dialogue is how the diction and syntax are used when the characters are speaking. There's lots of dialogue in this Companion book too. Do you find it realistic or perhaps even revealing in some way? Dialogue takes tone into consideration and characters have different tones as they speak depending on the subject or the emotions called for. What are your thoughts about the dialogue and do the virtuals speak any differently than the humans do?

Irony: what did you think of The Writer expressing her feelings about seeing her own work up on the Stardust String of Stories? Did you ever consider the feelings of a character in literature and where those feelings come from?

Foreshadowing: Our goal is to enlighten you about many literary devices and elements of literature. Of course we can't consider all of them, but since we had so much discussion about foreshadowing, what do you think about its use and consequences? Did it keep you on your toes?

There's so much more to consider. Answering these questions and thinking about literary devices helps you when you read your next book, and the one after that, and so on. Eventually you become a master at seeing through the episodes, the chapters, and even the lines of a story.

It's good to become a master reader, an investigator of all things fictional. I love the stuff and hope some ideas open up any box in your mind in case the literary lid is on too tight. Open up, find out, and let stardust words of explanation about literary devices be a light of discovery as you read.

End of ACT II, Scene Two

Notes, Images, Creative Thoughts

Notes, Images, Creative Thoughts

You've been invited for a big reveal.
Heads up.
Here it comes.

Intermission

Pages 124 - 130

As the white lights are dimmed, a narrow, bright golden spotlight travels along a winding path that hugs the edge of the stage. The Chorus of four virtuals are walking under its path as the aura begins to glow again in the background.

The Chorus is considering that they have reached a climactic moment. No, there is no foreshadowing about to be revealed. What the Chorus is going to reveal is why the book was innovative.

The four virtuals tell the audience in unison that,

CHORUS

The mother of the Author, who in the story is known by her adoring neighbors as Malone, is actually the reason both the book was written and why people are intrigued by it. There is a mystery embedded as to how a story like this could come about.

The mystery disentangles at this point and will unravel in ACT III as the Chorus discloses that this good and kind woman holds the Secret of Stardust in her heart.

CHORUS

The secret was partly disclosed in the children's series, then again in the trilogy: *Star Girl, The Secret of Stardust,* and *A Gathering of Stardust,* and *The Girl*

Who Invented Stardust. Now Malone's virtual offspring are bound to proclaim in this City Brick Memoir Series the very near miracle of her goodness. Stay tuned for ACT III.

When a person like Malone, a Queen of goodness and joy, is born into the world it is cause for celebration. Books and all kinds of honorifics for people like her are all too rare. Therefore, her story must be told by us, the Chorus.

Cleve steps out in front of the Chorus and says,

CLEVE

It bears repeating that, "A story is a walk you take with the story's author along a mystic street. As you walk, your imagination and The Writer's imagination become one. The stardust in the reader and in The Writer finds its way into each other's hearts, and they fold into someone new…."

As we read the story of the Queen of Goodness and Joy, Cleve says that it compels us to pull down the light from the stars and use it to keep our spirit bright. Cleve continues through several paragraphs of the script, narrating some of the most beautiful, heartfelt and inspirational lines of the book.

Cleve blushes, honored to be the virtual chosen to inform the audience that the Queen's gift of goodness and joy came to her by walking in harmony with the stars, a metaphor for walking in peace and love. He says so eloquently,

"The star girl, born in the simplicity of a brick row house in the Kerry Patch of North St. Louis, among the poorest of the Irish immigrants, was given the gift of starlight that still reflects hope in the eyes of all who walk inside her story."

The aura becomes brighter and brighter as Cleve steps back in line with the rest of the Chorus. They all hold each other's hands as they continue down the path remembering their Walk With A Star Girl Who Became A Queen.

Notes, Images, Creative Thoughts

ACT III

Pages 131 –188

The Workshop audience is buzzing about the idea of Star Girl, and Cleve asks them to settle back in their seats. The stagehands are busy moving the Knowing Trees into position. They have placed them in a row and are weaving a rope in and out between their trunks.

The Author and The Writer appear on stage. They clasp hands and hold up their arms signaling a sign of victory. The Author speaks first.

AUTHOR

You will remember that Myay's mother, who you know as the Queen, told Myay on page 133 that the tops of the pines are like ink pens and they write across the sky when the breeze blows.

Simulating a breeze, the stage hands begin fanning one of the trees using huge leaves made of bamboo. The tree is none other than the ancient Methuselah Pine. A sign is lowered into its tree tops and words begin to appear on the sign that say, "I not only talk; I also write across the sky."

A snare drum is heard like a rumble of thunder. Then the Pine Tree bends forward.

THE PINE

I am the great Pinus Strobus. I write prayers across the sky. Why? I fancy myself a prickly shield, and I can wield a needle like an arrow, like the magician Prospero. If anyone dares mess with Me--thuselah, or Myay, they will hear me say as I pray that I am the Superman of trees. I write with the breeze and implore The Keeper of Trees to keep my needles strong and pointy. Please! I'm in the business of defense, hence I must be a strong and lean green machine -- to watch over the Queen.

AUTHOR

Well that was a thunderous welcome to ACT III. We thank the Pine Tree for such gallant protection and gorgeous wood that the stagehands use to build beautiful stages like this. I might add, we are grateful to all The Knowing Trees who are on our team, for they give us so much. And speaking of team, The Writer and I are teaming up to present this Act.

Together we hope to generate more discussion about interesting literary topics that may not have come to the fore in Book I. We hope this will bolster an already dynamic reader and study guide. In honor of Myay's obvious influence on Pinus Strobus I say let the script rip!

Cleve is standing back in the shadows, leaning against a tree trunk and looking quizzical. He addresses the Author.

Cleve

Well, you're sounding playful. But I must ask, is it just you two on the team and you're leaving Iris out of this buddy presentation? In the last scene you both got a wee bit testy with each other. You as Author are non-fiction and The Writer, like me, is fiction. Ahem, I mean virtual.

The audience will catch on to your unlikely new simpatico and hold you two to the prosaic fire if you don't explain her absence here and now. Can you clarify?

AUTHOR

I was prepared for the audience's questions, Cleve, but you too? You should know better.

The Writer

Let me take this one please. We are not leaving Iris out of anything, Cleve. We are gratefully using Iris's research and ideas to make this guide more instructive and interactive. Iris is our literary archeologist and she has dug into the plot of Myay's story.

Her inspiration is why we chose the title, *Threads Beyond The Text.* Her will to pursue what lies below the surface of a story is why this script will bring a new angle to Myay's story – and her own.

You know, Cleve, this fiction/non-fiction duet we're singing is not regular. If the Author were talking to a truly fictional character, that would be dicey enough. But hey, she is talking to me. In essence, she is talking to herself, in the past, present and sometimes future tense.

That bridges the great divide between fiction and non-fiction, between real and virtual, and the barriers of time. Mirroring these traditional opposites creates a brand new view of what's possible in a range of literary options that haven't been tested. We all thought you understood that Cleve.

CLEVE

Well, you thought I understood your theory of stardust until you found out my questions showed a total lack of understanding and believability. But you have to admit that my questions serve a purpose. They force both of you into clarifications you may not have otherwise felt the need to explain. I would bet the audience and the readers feel the same. This new literary territory you're testing is tricky with tough turf at times.

There comes a burst of applause from the audience, obviously in thanks to Cleve for his inquiries.

THE WRITER

Point taken and I hope things progress more smoothly because we're all on the same page. Another unintended pun, but appropriate. And by the way, Cleve, we are inviting Iris to be our *special* guest and reveal the hidden themes she has found in Book I.

CLEVE

She's not a guest; she's one of us, but I'll let that slide for now, because I have to interrupt this team broadcast to focus on the unique visual that the stagehands have created. Set your eyes on the rope that is weaving its way through the trees. Iris, my better fourth, is a teacher and she says visuals work miracles when explaining literary terms that pertain to a story.

She says some literary terms are off-putting so we thought we would highlight one that is prominent in *The Shelter of Trees*. We want to clarify how a certain literary device is used, so readers do not have to question why certain text is presented repeatedly. Thus, we will start with the *trope*, a term some people may not be fully acquainted with. As Iris informs the listening and reading public, I'll be the one trying to keep up. But I'm still a little peeved that you called her a guest, because that makes me part of the visiting team too. And you two are the home team?

THE WRITER

Try to relax, Cleve. You are misinterpreting my use of the word guest. I'm sorry, but your misunderstanding gives us another literary device to explain. I won't go off on a tangent about the various types of irony, yet you've been caught up in one type and that's called verbal irony.

It happens in literature, Cleve, when there is confusion between what is said and what is meant. Actually, I meant to compliment Iris by calling her a guest. Guests are usually treated with great respect due to their status as a friend, or relation, or special person who brings blessings to the world. Iris is all those things to us and more, Cleve. Rest assured.

CLEVE

It's just that I'm supposed to keep an eye on my virtual family and I'm becoming anxious, like I'm going to lose one of you. I suppose I just overreact at times.

THE WRITER

What makes you think you're going to lose one of us, Cleve?

CLEVE

I'm not sure. I just feel it rumbling beyond the text like a trope *who* is so taut it's about to snap.

THE WRITER

Oh Cleve, why would you say *who*? Tropes aren't real; they are imaginary.

CLEVE

My dear Writer, that sounds a lot like the pot calling the virtual kettle black? I was right about one thing, new literary territory can be tricky.

Cleve is feeling hacked.

He is a virtual
High-Tech Wreck.

THE WRITER

We love the way you care for us, Cleve. I am happy you are the clever quarter of our self. Don't be nervous about moving from the prose of our books to this dialogue. Yes, it's a challenge, but together we can pull it off. I've followed Iris' research and I want to help her bring new understanding of literary terms that will give writers the confidence to use them.

You know our goal is to be companion writers and help others find their own stardust words. This discussion gives us a tremendous opportunity to shed light on some slick techniques. So let's get *cyber-literary* and start with a constructive critique of the Author's use of something important in stories that we call tropes.

The Writer points to the trees as Cleve calls an audible.

CLEVE

Wait, wait, wait, cyber-literary? You're already moving too fast for me.

THE WRITER

Cyber-literary is when you get in to this stuff so much that it's second nature, and fiction is more real than not. Human authors who create virtual characters merge in the same way you said a reader and an author does. The writing of fiction moves from inside the author's mind and hits the page in real time. It's powerful and the reader subtly feels a lightness of being, as two minds are immersed in the author's story. It's losing your body to a state of mind, something like meditation. It's also something like being in *The Shelter of Cool Confidence.*

Tropes help make that happen. They are literary devices that keep a reader in that suspended state of bliss. A tropes is being illustrated by the rope you see looping its way in and out of the trees. The rope/trope metaphorically ties the trees together in a way. A trope is a repetitive idea that loops through a plot and holds a story together.

This rope visual shows you how it works. Take the story of the Knowing Trees. It weaves in and out of the text. So, a trope is a kind of storytelling device that helps to keep a plot moving, yet holds it together at the same time. It's the yarn that is knitting its way forward while keeping the garment in one piece. Now the Author will give you some examples of tropes she used to hold Myay's story together.

The trees begin to move and shake to get the audience to look at them. The Author nears the trees and holds on to the rope as she walks along it, weaving her way in and out of the trees.

AUTHOR

So The Writer mentioned that the Knowing Trees themselves are a trope in the strict sense of the word. Their wisdom is full of goodness. They serve as authority figures who hold the story to a higher standard as they keep the reader interested in their thought-provoking dialogue.

Also, as the plot of the five books progresses, it becomes clear that Myay's Quest to reach her aunt's flat in North St. Louis is also a trope. Her pursuit intrigues the reader who wants to find out if she will actually make it.

THE WRITER

Those are strong tropes and your use of stardust which subtly debuts in the mud of Myay's backyard is yet another trope. It acts like a framework for everything in the story that is good. I would further suggest that goodness itself is a trope. It holds the story together because each and every character can be counted on to have good intentions.

So goodness also runs through the plot like a rope, keeping the characters true to their convictions. They demonstrate their desire to be writing companions, ready to assist writers in any way they possibly can. And they never deviate from this commitment. Iris can you shed some light on our discussion of the use of tropes? And then explain the difference in tropes and themes that you find in the story?

The spotlight centers on Iris who is sitting at a desk with books and a pile of papers. The trees are bowing again of course. They usually overreact when she's around.

Iris

I must begin with a disclaimer. This story is lacking one trope and that is the use of good and evil to influence the plot. The author would not allow the use of evil in our story and that's fine by us. And here's something else. The use of a rope to exemplify a trope that holds a story together can also have the opposite effect.

I refer you to the cover of this guide. You see the rope shown is a means to a contradictory end. It can unfurl and subsequently liberate. Ropes are as good as the threads from which they are made. Although often unintended, some unravel and set free what they were supposed to be holding.

They can go too far as a result of not being appropriate in the first place. They can go beyond the text, disappearing on an off ramp because they can't hold tight due to the tension of hidden sub-plots that tear at them.

A sub-plot, be it explicit or hidden, is a powerful literary device that adds dramatic tension to the story.

Cleve reaches his arms out to the audience in a you-see-what-I-mean pose.

CLEVE

This is why I have to listen closely. Are you saying a trope doesn't always hold?

IRIS

Yes, it's only as strong as the writer's intended use of it. It's going to sound odd, but I am one of the tropes in *The Shelter of Trees*. I keep showing up in several of the Author's stories, Cleve. As a literary archeologist, I dig into stories to find underlying themes that might be festering due to sub-plots. I've gotten pretty good at connecting fantasy and history, because I dig so deeply I can see where they cross into each other's territory.

Knowing where they cross paths, I can link imagery and facts taking readers into a zone that is away from reality and into the spectacular space of the imagination. That's a cyber-literary ride on the Enlightenment, Cleve,

Like description, imagery uses vivid and figurative language, metaphors, and similes to appeal to the reader's senses.

CLEVE

I'm hanging in there with all of the information you are explaining in between the lines of this script.

IRIS

Good, don't let go of the rope, Cleve, as I explain that the Author's personality is a prism of which each of us virtuals is one side. My role has been to research the power that stardust has inside of us. I absolutely love doing this, and unexpectedly, discovered that its power is in other objects, like trees and brick of course, that we thought to be inanimate.

I should have known of course that stardust elements are in wood and clay, and that these once thought inanimates have stories too. Where possibility and reality meet is the heart of a cyber-literary nexus. But Cleve, take nothing for granted for it can snap at any time from too much tension.

Stardust as a prime mover has been a breathtaking discovery for me. Before I began my research or touched the keyboard, it was written that I should learn this. It's the circuit that Emily Dickinson refers to in her poem, *Success In Circuit Lies*. I was written into literature to be a part of the same creative process that allows me to write stardust words.

The stardust words go round and round like a wheel of fortune until an epiphany occurs and they stop abruptly so an idea can form, an idea like me or you. This happens phenomenally, inexplicably in the cyberspace of a writer's mind. Writing creatively with stardust words powers discovery and progress.

CLEVE

So I am an idea?. I feel like more than that, but that's your take on the story of literary creation. I mean a certain kind of creation. I know you love to research, Iris, but where did you learn about all things cyber-literary?

The audience is paying strict attention. You could hear a rope drop.

A character born of stardust is
the legacy of the Queen who
points the way to
The Land of Goodness and Joy

So this is what's going on!

IRIS

Where I learned this has an easy answer, Cleve. I learned it where I lived. You've been hearing about a Star Girl in the pages of the book in a fantastic sort of way. There's another side to every Star Girl. A Star Girl lives like the Author through many ages and phases and even many names at times.

I have been in almost every story the Author has created. I fell from the sky in her book entitled *Star Girl*, I appeared on stage with The Writer in her play *A Gathering of Stardust*, I taught a class in her novella, *The Girl Who Invented Stardust.* I've been around, Cleve.

I have existed inside of Myay in *The Shelter of Trees. I am a descendent of Hanna* who sailed from Ireland in the belly of a boat, and from her daughter, Malone, who lived in the Kerry Patch of North St. Louis, I am Iris, the virtual manifestation who is with you right here in *Threads Beyond The Text.*

Don't faint on me, Cleve. We don't know what your history is. It could be even more intriguing than mine. This guide book is about more than one Coming of Age story. I am called on once again to continue my work. I began as a young Star Girl teaching children about the harmony that exists among constellations.

Now I'm bringing the concept down to earth through Myay, a character with a fantastic history who the Author hopes will help turn the real world into The

Land of Goodness and Joy. Luckily, we all like big challenges, Cleve.

CLEVE

I do actually feel a little faint.

IRIS

Come on, my clever fourth, don't fall apart on me. This isn't a magic act I'm referring to. Creative writing enters the portals of deep thought like black holes and pulls out fantastic, new ways to arrange stardust words that become fantastic, new ideas. These mental portals are doors to those moments just before discovery. I assume that by now you know a metaphor when you hear one, Cleve.

This is one reason ACT III is heavy on explaining literary devices so that the audience, the readers, and especially writers learn the ropes and master the use of literary tools. It builds proficiency to know everything that is useful and good about your craft. But that's exactly it, isn't it? Writing for the sake of goodness is the vessel that lets us into the portal.

In this book's context, I grew up as Myay, a well- read young adult who wanted to shed her childhood, yet not give it up completely. I understand her need to follow her heart and never give up, and to stay on the trail of stardust. I empathize with the wide-eyed enthusiasm of her youth – and mine. How can I accomplish my goal unless I keep at it? Cyber-literary devices let a girl like me stay in the "real" world.

She gives Cleve a wry smile.

It's been remarked that Myay's character has been seen as too old for her years, that it was always me and not her creating quotes, poems, and humorous scenarios. But she did exist. She just sensed somehow, before she was me, that what was buried in the mud of her backyard, and in the clay of St. Louis soil would form exquisite brick. It's a phenom, but her psychology was deep as was her perception. She sensed things, and you may understand that just from having been young yourself. You were young once, weren't you, Cleve?

CLEVE

They tell me I was, although I don't remember life before the City Brick Memoir Series.

IRIS

Call on your stardust, Cleve. Myay knew the stardust elements of her memory could bring her beloved Kielys back to her. She knew if she concentrated deeply she would see Hannah and The Cailleach and many of the Disadvantaged Royalty that she never had a chance to meet in "real" life. Oh yes stardust was a very powerful trope in *The Shelter of Trees*.

And that trope led to her quest. Myay never gave up trying to track stardust to the end of the rainbow. And eventually the rainbow appeared over her brick palace at 3022a Kossuth in Old North St. Louis. It was more than a four-family flat, it was an elegant edifice of the Disadvantaged Royalty. It ranks among the famous houses of literature, and I'm here to proclaim it as such.

Myay read every word that Jane Austin ever wrote. And knew of her famous estates at Pemberly, Northanger Abbey and Mansfield Park. She was mesmerized by the grandeur of Daphne Du Maurier's Manderley in *Rebecca*, and Bronte's gloomy Thornfield Hall of *Jane Eyre* fame. These estates were etched in her imagination and she felt that her aunt's Palace of Brick was no less stately. The trope of Myay's house is the background of each book cover in the City Brick Memoir Series. Don't doubt that it's been stunning and very creative writing that brought the famous houses of literature to life, Cleve.

CLEVE

I swear I won't. In fact I wouldn't dare. Can you leave the houses and go into the yard where I assume you dig up the many themes that surround stories like Myay's?

IRIS

Of course, you are getting quite figurative yourself, Cleve. The theme of Myay's aunt's house, her four-family flat actually, that runs throughout the whole series, is one of shelter. The Palace of Brick was a "fairer house than prose" and much more so than her Hansel and Gretel house in Jennings; that's for sure.

Themes, my stock in trade, are different than tropes. Themes lurk and linger in a story and must be drawn out. They provide meaning and bear important messages for readers, often as moral takeaways. The image you see that introduces ACT III is a clear illustration of a trope as a strong rope, in this case a rope holding the Knowing Trees together.

Themes that arise are more subtle, almost transparent at times. They are more like silken threads that hold the Knowing Trees together rather than the strong, brown hemp of rope. A trope can be obvious, whereas the theme may be buried in the text like stardust is buried in rich clay mud.

Let's take Myay's neighborhood of Jennings. It was made up of kind neighbors, homes, stores, churches, schools and businesses, all working together to make Myay's life glorious and filled with opportunity. It points up a special theme that The Writer and the Author want to emphasize. It's the importance of teamwork that comes from a supportive network. It can even take the place of an extended family.

I could write a whole book on how the humans, the virtuals, and the Knowing Trees worked together and shared their stardust in good ways to give Myay prospects for a better life. This is the kind of teamwork that will evolve the world into The Land of Goodness and Joy.

And speaking of that light-filled paradise, there's the theme of light or call it illumination if you choose. It comes from getting in touch with the goodness in your own heart, your Stardust Chamber. It allows you to see beyond the dark and to achieve great things when you connect to its goodness.

The businesses of Jennings were a lifeline to Myay. The church and school provided her academic and spiritual education. The neighbors were her support system, and us virtuals who climbed out of her intellect helped her write her story, while the Kielys and Malones gave her the confidence to pursue her dreams.

Myay grew intellectually so quickly that I had to come out. Thus, the coming of age trope led to the theme of character influence. I was destined to become a teacher because of the example and influence of my network of supporters. I was compelled to find ways to give back the gifts I was given.

And while I have the stage, I must mention another theme, that of perseverance. It's the meaning inherent in Myay's striving to never let a negative get in the way of staying on the trail of stardust that begins to germinate in Book I. She strives throughout the series to overcome unspoken negative obstacles at the Hansel and Gretel house, to follow her dreams that will take her to--wait for it, Cleve,

CLEVE

I know, to The Land of Goodness and Joy.

IRIS

The neighbors in Jennings persevered and nurtured each other in ways that helped Myay and themselves live life without an emphasis on material goods. Perseverance is a necessity for the middle class. Perseverance is why the Knowing Trees could weather the winter's ice and cold, and the summer's heat and storms. The trees know, and always knew, that persevering is the way to Begin Again.

I refer you to the image on page 189 of *The Shelter of Trees*. It illustrates the children persevering as they work together to nourish the tree, and it correlates to the theme of beginning again. Every time they tended to the tree they began a new cycle of life for themselves and the tree.

So to our dear audience, to you, Cleve, and those out there listening and reading along with us, I hope I was clear on the difference in the meaning of tropes and themes. Let my words reach you like stardust wafting in moonbeams as you dream of the Land of Goodness and Joy. Myay lives!

AUTHOR

I guess we know where that came from Iris. You still have Myay's 3D Poetry in you. In this interactive workshop, we are now going to ask our audience to write down other tropes they think held the story together and other themes they believe can be derived from the story.

Notes, Images, Creative Thoughts

The audience rumbles audibly in excitement and quickly begins to write as Cleve is busy handing out clothes pins. After writing out their thoughts, they're asked to come up on stage and pin what they wrote to the rope.

Then they are to take turns using the small pocket knife on the table next to the Chinese Elm to carve their initials. When the papers are pinned and the initials carved, the audience returns to their seats feeling like bonafide members of the cast.

Cleve thanks Iris for helping everyone understand what the reader's guide is all about. He informs the audience that the Director is considering overtime for the stagehands. The audience responds with cheers as Myay walks out on stage.

MYAY

Dear audience, you have made this gathering a success, just as the support of the good neighbors in Jennings made my pursuit of stardust a success. They helped my family thrive in that little Hansel and Gretel House. I grew with their care and that of the teachers of St. Louis De Marillac. They were The Daughters of Charity who believed in me and allowed me to study French at their college on the Marillac campus. Merci, merci!

And the Confectionary and Drug Store were not just neighborhood businesses, they were my own personal enrichment centers where I learned to socialize and grow in mindfulness and knowledge. Their example not only sustained me with food and fun, and magazines and books, it led me to a life of inquiry, trying to find the stardust words that would give back to the world what it gave me.

THE WRITER

Thank you, Myay, we can count on you to share the deepest parts of yourself. Now, we'll get back to our team presentation. We hope this guide has given you a better understanding of the literary techniques used in a story that make a reader amazed, astounded, stunned, and startled. Nothing electrifies like stardust words that lift us out of this world and into the one where the angels are funny fireflies. If you get my lift?

AUTHOR

So as not to give our Director a nervous breakdown I'm going to list some remaining episodes and ask you in the audience to vote on which of them you would like to hear about. So here's the list:

> The Daughters of Charity, the Mother House, the Confectionary, the Yellow Jacket and the Neighbor Ladies, the YMCA and the Near Drowning Incident, the Drug Store with its magnificent spinning magazine rack, more about all the trees that accompany those episodes which are the Catalpa, the Cherry, the Apple, the Weeping Willow, the Ceiba, the Tree of Heaven, the Christmas Tree, and the Tree of Light. We can review

these, or do you want to hear new material that lets you in on what happens in the rest of the story? Majority rules and we will honor your wishes.

Cleve collects the votes from the audience and counts them . The audience was nearly unanimous in wanting to hear a little about each one and the rest of the story too. The Director is heard sighing heavily as he stands in the dark at the back of the stage.

DIRECTOR

All right, I can't go that far, but I won't deny you a grand finale to this trailblazing drama. I confess that I too have enjoyed this time together, I would like to know the rest of the story. I would even like to get to know Iris, so I'm approving extra time for a Finale. I suppose if the good sisters were here they would say I'm becoming a convert.

The audience gives the Director a standing ovation.

The audience calls for an interview with Iris to get more questions answered!!!

Ask me no questions
I'll tell you no lies

Well that's not gonna work in this Workshop!

INTERVIEW WITH IRIS

The last time Iris turned the tables and asked questions of the audience. Now Cleve is suggesting that Iris sit for an interview so that the audience can get the rest of their questions answered.

AUDIENCE MEMBER

Style: You say this is creative writing, so how is it different from regular writing?

IRIS

It's not too different really, but it may take a little longer to get to the finish line. Personally, if I have an idea that I think is worth pursuing, I give it an awful lot of thought trying to change it from something mundane into something new, something that crosses boundaries like metaphors do and like poetry does. The process is way more exciting.

AUDIENCE MEMBER

The Setting: I thought the setting was interesting, but I would have liked to have more scenery. Why did you only depict The Knowing Trees of Jennings when there were so many other tropes and themes you could have illustrated with props?

IRIS

The Author believes in the importance of trees. That's why she began her writing career by creating a character from the rainforest. Trees as partners can help us stop climate change if only we would let them thrive. It's a personal choice to trust in trees to do that, because every partnership has to be built on trust. They were given the full stage to show how much we believe in them.

AUDIENCE MEMBER

The Characters: The virtuals blew me away. Why did the Author speak through them in *The Shelter of Trees* and in this book too?

IRIS

That's a question for the Author, and if my intuition is corrcct the answer may become apparent in the Finale. We all have foils of some kind, but we virtuals do not contrast with the Author as foils would.

Foil is a literary device that allows for contrast between the protagonist and another character. A good example is Sherlock Holmes' skill at reasoning compared to Dr. Watson's powers of observation.

I suppose we virtuals could be called author surrogates because we stand in for the author. She created us to bring a distance between herself and reality. That's as much as I can say.

AUDIENCE MEMBER

The Plot: I don't know how I could write my way into a plot like this. Got any suggestions?

IRIS

Yes, I have many. I'll begin by saying that you should read Books II and III of the City Brick Memoir Series. It will give you the confidence you need to proceed without the insecurity of feeling like writing, in any way, is above your capability. It's not. If you can write a sentence about yourself, you can write a paragraph about yourself. Then you can read over the paragraph and determine where to insert your own name. When you do that to even a small piece of writing you take ownership. You have the deed to your writing and nobody can take it from you. Give it a try.

AUDIENCE MEMBER

Tone: Whose tone strikes you as the most convincing? I know you are involved in creating the dialogue, but I also imagine that you have your personal preferences too. If it's too hard to be objective, I apologize.

IRIS

No, it's not too hard. It's just that I can't quite compare, because I'm never sure what my own tone sounds like. When it comes to someone else's in the cast, I would say it's Cleve. He makes no bones about who he is and what he thinks and it comes through in the tone of his dialogue. Just ask him and he'll probably tell you how genuine and true his tone is.

AUDIENCE MEMBER

Conflict: I've read that a plot should be dynamic. The plot of Myay's story wouldn't be described like that. How would you describe it and would the inclusion of more conflict have made it dynamic?

IRIS

Well, I don't think so. I'm not a fan of conflict any which way. Even when I teach a story that has conflict it makes me a bit nervous. I know that very learned critics think conflict can make or break a story and they know more than me. As a matter of personal preference, however, I would rather spend my time engaging in stories that bring joy not anxiety.

AUDIENCE MEMBER

Narration: I had to stay tuned in order to keep pace with the many narrators. Was that intentional on your part to keep us on our toes? Why four different voices or should I say phases?

IRIS

Yes it was intentional and call us what you will. I am part of one life that has been led over the years. I represent the Author's peak time of life. I also represent her insecurity and her compassion. I cared for Myay until I made my debut, and I cared enough for the rest of the world to dedicate myself to education. I'm proud of that, but I can only legitimately speak to one age, one phase. You have been exposed to all others also in a creative way.

AUDIENCE MEMBER

Point of View: Is there another point of view being heard that is not identified? It feels like there is.

IRIS

Yes, and I can't identify it either because it is almost inaudible yet bubbling up from the sub-plot in some way. I don't necessarily mean there is another narrator, but I'm pretty sure there is another point of view to be heard before we end.

AUDIENCE MEMBER

Genre: As a member of the audience, I love the idea of being a participating character. I wish I had a bigger role. Will interactive literary opportunities go viral?

IRIS

The books of City Brick Memoir Series are considered historical fiction. They are written in 3D poetry and prose. This dramatic format is close to the same, but we want it to be more educational than entertaining. To me they sort of both merge in a new experience that let's an onlooker like you become a part of the story. It's a dynamic that is not reflected in conflict but in creativity. We are so glad you enjoyed taking an active part. So if I say it could go viral, you'll have to go with it.

The audience laughs.

AUDIENCE MEMBER

Trope: What was your favorite trope of the whole story, or I guess I mean which one did you enjoy writing about the most?

IRIS

It has to do with me, but if I say too much I might give away more than the Author wants me to. I can say that my favorite is Myay's quest. It's not only a quest to find out the trail that stardust took to get here. It's a quest to find its trail into her heart. And once found, to decide what to do with that knowledge.

I mean whether or not to act on its power to strengthen her individuality, to help her live the life she was capable of living. This is hard. I can't discount the trope of stardust either. It's in all things, even our conscience, which is why we know it to be a prime mover. I guess I have several favorite tropes.

AUDIENCE MEMBER

Theme: Do you think every stardust seeker finds his or her shelter in life?

IRIS

Sadly, no I don't. Love is a shelter that we all deserve, but some have very little of it or none at all. Finding love is a universal theme because it shelters us from the sadness of being alone. I do believe everyone seeks it, even if they don't know they are. A tree bends toward the light and the rest of us reach for the starlight, the source of love, goodness, and joy. Starlight has never failed to shelter us.

AUDIENCE MEMBER

Symbolism: What are all the things a shelter means to you?

IRIS

The title, *The Shelter of Trees,* should tell you a lot. Of course, a tree is a shelter from the sun and from an earth that can become too dry and arid. A neighborhood is a shelter of community, faith is a shelter from fear, a house is a shelter for family and relationships.

I would add that an education is a shelter of social security, and then there's a special shelter that I had which was The Shelter of City Brick, one of protection, peace and safety.

I hope I answered your questions to your satisfaction. Let me know what you think of our interview.

END OF ACT III

Notes, Images, Creative Thoughts

Notes, Images, Creative Thoughts

The Finale

Book Pages 189 – 216

The stagehands are murmuring. They just can't understand why the rope they erected is beginning to fray.

The Director appears saying the discussion of the book's ending episodes will be cut short. He tells the audience they are experiencing an emergency with the rope prop and it will have to be fixed – somehow.

He specifically apologizes to the special guests that attended a play entitled A Gathering of Stardust. They were none other than the Pharmacist, the Minister, the Scientist, the Skeptic, Sherlock, the Interlocutor and Rosemary. Neither the author nor the cast knew they were the ones asking the questions, because the foot lights kept the audience in the dark.

And now the stage is dark too except for one tree and a damaged rope. The stagehands have placed a large image of the cover of this Reader's Guide on the stage that illustrates Myay leaping off the roof of her aunt's flat. They prop up a ladder and what's left of the rope on the illustration as the lights brighten over the Author and Iris.

IRIS

Where's Cleve and The Writer? I thought we would all appear together in this last scene.

AUTHOR

They said they wanted to yield back their time to you. It's the right thing to do because you've been short changed a bit before this series. You were anonymous in *Star Girl.* Although you appeared in *A Gathering of Stardust* and *The Girl Who Invented Stardust,* it wasn't until your role as Myay's older self that you could reveal your literary gifts. Who are you really, Iris?

IRIS

Well, if you don't know…

Sorry, that sounded smart, but really we both know I'm the longest living part of you, you the woman of many names. You are all of us virtuals combined. In what some call the real world you are Malone's daughter, Molly. To your students you are Mrs. Bunton, as a writer you are M. Catherine Bunton, and now as a character you are The Author. And you ask me who I am?

Pseudonym is a name used instead of a real name.

AUTHOR

Looks like I've spread myself pretty thin.

IRIS

There's a reason, but being only one part of you I can't say why that is. If you ever were a child, really, I carried your inquiring mind into young adulthood, into me, and I grasped at every literary straw I could find to stay balanced.

Your readers could see that Myay's quest to reach her aunt's flat in North St. Louis was half genuine and half pretense. Her quest, in part, was her constant hope for some intellectual or physical diversion that would take her away. That need stayed with her later when she began to write. She had to find a way out of the anxiety that led to incoherent first drafts when she wrote.

Her brilliant teachers knew from the disorganization of her essays that she suffered from an emotional disconnect. She needed to find some way out of a state that had her trapped in confusion, and into a place of clarity that would allow her to write intelligibly. Because she couldn't find it, she had to create it.

The Author looks curious, almost fascinated.

I guess it's why you chose fiction as your specialty. Only there could you find a world of possibility that would offer you a way out of confusion. You always looked for a diversion, but you were tethered to this world by an anchor of anxiety and hesitation, so you tried fleeing reality and using your stardust words as a way out.

AUTHOR

Well, Iris, I am intrigued. Since you are a literary archeologist, you seem to have uncovered my Escape Route, which I suppose I knew would be revealed in this Finale.

IRIS

Your words have kept you hostage, and, as you say, they will also set you free. The hidden theme of this memoir is obvious. You are still on a journey that began in Jennings under cover of us virtuals and The Knowing Trees. You are still making your way toward the end of a rainbow that really didn't end at the Palace of Brick.

Withholding is a narrative technique whereby a writer keeps crucial information from the reader.

We've all been on the trail with you, but the journey hasn't been easy for any of us. You cleverly hid the story of the "wavy boards" of the Hansel and Gretel House, and the reason for your desire to get to Aunties. It wasn't just for the pure joy of it, it was a life line to something stable and safe.

AUTHOR

It's fine for you to expose the route I took, Iris, but not the downside of my life. If I wanted to do that I would have.

IRIS

You would have? No. You couldn't. You needed the cover of all the virtual parts of you. Even with us you were hardly able to expose tiny hints. I won't say anymore if you don't want me to. I'll let your conscience be your guide. Mine tells me that anymore of this conversation has to come from you.

AUTHOR

Oh heavens, Iris, you are my conscience too. I grapple with all of you every day. If I knew why I couldn't reveal the story of what happened on Helen Avenue at the Hansel and Gretel House maybe the book, the play, and this Finale, wouldn't be necessary.

IRIS

Probably it would not, but you've been too afraid. You're still afraid of your own memories, of hurting others even if they're dead, and of coming down off a pedestal.

AUTHOR

Off a pedestal? Wow. I don't think I'm that proud.

IRIS

Think again. Wasn't the upsetting circumstances of your young life an embarrassment? Of course they were, so wasn't it just better to sweep them under the rug as you sometimes did with your mother's advice? That's why your five-book memoir is nothing but goodness and joy. Of course, that's not a bad thing, but on the truth scale it doesn't measure up. You had to be a savior for your family, a standout that they could hang on to in order to keep the lid on.

AUTHOR

The lid, yes. To keep the lid on a pot boiling with disdain was fairly common. I suppose it's all true, but I didn't set out to write an autobiography. City Brick is a memoir and I don't have to reveal every aspect of my life. I mean there's so many sad, whiny memoirs. One of the first I ever read was one that my sister owned. It was Lillian Helman's *Ill cry Tomorrow.* I do wonder now why she had that book? Anyway, I wanted my memoir to be happy.

IRIS

Well, excuses will only get you so far. We've published the joyful parts in the first five books. But this Finale is your one chance to bring out another part. You created me to explore hidden themes in stories; was it because subconsciously you wanted the truth to come out eventually? I don't have to dig up embarrassing moments, but I should be charged with getting at the truth. And the truth is something you've always told writers was at the end of the evolutionary writing process. Seems you would want to back that up with some real world evidence.

AUTHOR

Yes, so it seems. But it's easier said than done for me, yet I know I don't have much time to think about it. The Director is already clamoring that we won't finish before the audience has to leave.

IRIS

I don't think they will leave at all. They have unanswered questions and if we answer them in the script of this Finale they will leave satisfied not disgruntled over bcing kept in the dark.

The Author sighs deeply.

AUTHOR

If I do this, everyone will have to listen, especially you. If you say anything I might lose my nerve and back out. I also want to be able to say "CUT" at any time.

IRIS

As if you couldn't? We all need to "CUT" the drama. You can do whatever you want to do and we won't say a word. But I know you know that.

It seems you subconsciously wrote two stories at once as many authors do. One storyline appears in the text of your lively historical fiction, while the other is somewhere beyond it, or buried in it.

Finding what's buried in the text is my stock in trade. As your literary archeologist, you know I can help you reveal what you've hidden. It will bring a new perspective to your story. In some ways it's only fair to give the listeners and readers that understanding.

Three dots that indicate an omission of thought.

AUTHOR

Well before I do anything drastic…

IRIS

It's not drastic.

AUTHOR

I'm feeling unsettled as if what I could be leading up to just might be drastic. So, let's talk a bit about a few of the last episodes. In the book they are filled with big ideas that I know the audience wants to re-view.

Iris agrees and lifts up a sign she had been holding behind her back. It says, "Heaven was a place called Marillac."

IRIS

I want to start with Marillac, an episode I was so glad to be part of. Marillac is where the Daughters of Charity lived and prayed and attended college on their campus. I was sent to Marillac, The Mother House, when I was Myay. Those days with the nuns, perfecting my French and exploring the grounds, were bonus days.

Myay walks out on stage and asks Iris to remember when they would pile in the car with the nuns and head to Marillac for a day of learning and probably a little shenanigans too. The old Pine that had been moved to the back of the stage was heard chuckling, because he knew what Myay was going to relate next.

MYAY

I explored that brick castle just like I did Auntie's Palace of Brick; yes, every corner required investigation. One favorite place to explore was the underground tunnels that seemed to never end, a sprinter's dream. The tunnels were stucco and painted bright white. They were not dark like Auntie's hallway, still the lower realm could be treacherous if caught running at top speed.

When I was tired from running through the subterranean halls, a low down "s" word, hopefully unnoticed, I would make my way upstairs to the North end of the building which was the Villa where my dear retired nuns lived. It was a place that changed my career plan for the future.

The telling of this favorite episode inspired the spontaneous combustion of 3D Poetry. Overwhelmed with emotions from Myay's flashbacks of the pleasant days at Marillac, Iris recites her poem, Master of Ceremonies shown on page 150 of The Shelter of Trees.

Knowing Myay as you do by now, you know she never stops for long. She hugs Iris and tells her to perk up as she launches in to the episode on page 158 of The Shelter of Trees entitled, The Confectionary, her personal sweet shop.

MYAY

I remember my confectionary with its many "prizes" and ice cream, and candy apples. But I especially remember the penny candy.

As Myay starts to recite the yummy types of candy, the stage hands are walking through the aisles handing out red hots, dots, Slow Pokes and Charleston Chews, even fresh black and red licorice from Switzer's plant in St. Louis.

I loved to look around my tiny box of a store. It was like going to the Jennings flea market only sweeter.

There were more valuables at the confectionary than in Tutankhamen's tomb. I know that from many trips around the world in my favorite book. Bessy and Basil were the owners of the confectionary, and the queen and king of organization, perfecting this skill in a 6' x 14' treasure chest.

Myay wanted to carry on about the cherry tree with its polka dot red, and apple tree with green hanging fruit in Bessy and Basil's back yard. But there was no time; so she had to press on to her next narration. It's "a little story about a life-threatening occurrence that no God-Fearing child should ever have had to endure."

I was an innocent child, much like the famous Scout, when walking home from one of my several daily trips to Bessie and Basil's confectionary, I thought the day should be graced with a nice taste of the delicious honey suckle that lined their fence. Bad idea.

I was assaulted by a home invader, a Jennings street thug that wore a YELLOW JACKET. After being bitten I was like Tootie of *Meet Me In St. Louis* fame. I became the central focus of all the neighbor ladies who came to the rescue. The exciting uproar of the neighbors and attention from mom and brother Frank brought a reward, enough money to go back again.

The scene comes to an end as the stage hands roll out yet another Knowing Tree, the Weeping Willow known to have medicinal powers in its bark. A sign hanging in its branches said, "If Myay starts to give you a headache, come and see me and I'll give you an aspirin." Can you beat that?

AUTHOR

And just a few words about the Drug Store episode please. I want to mention that it was through the generosity of Ben Abel and his family that Myay was given her freedom to take off and fly. The Abel's had the hearts of philanthropists.

They gave her a new bike, and all the books, magazines, and comics, she could read. She was at Abel Drug every summer day reading everything they had, and the Abel's enjoyed having her around. Their generosity led to her lifelong interest in words, even those I write today.

And I must mention too the Tree of Heaven, highlighted on page 206, *Shelter of Trees*. It was a tree that grew out of the cracks of sidewalks in the City of St. Louis. Its name foreshadowed where Myay wanted to go. She said the tree was like her, "hard to control." Maybe that's why no one knew where she went at the end of *The Shelter of Trees.*

The Writer was happy, though, because she had been planning to take over in Books II and III. But the unpredictable Myay surfaces again in Book IV, old enough now to begin tracking how stardust got to Planet Earth. And in Book V she tracks it to her place of bliss where she was safe to dream.

The Myay that escaped early in the episode called *How I Became a Star Girl*, featured on page 73, well, she was never the same. It happened after an incident with a mirror that is not recounted in the book. I suppose the whole episode of an escape was a trope I devised for getting away from the anxiety and control of the Hansel and Gretel house.

So yes, there was family upset on Helen Avenue; there was disfunction and it sometimes overwhelmed a young girl born of love and kindness by a Queen called Malone. To Myay the chaotic circumstances that would spontaneously arise made no sense.

And I wasn't about to dwell on any of that. Besides, the memoir has been a successful attempt at uplifting and encouraging writers. This play has been another opportunity to offer information about how writing works with the help of tools. I guess you're right, there are two stories, maybe more.

IRIS

The audience will be grateful that you recapped the ending without sending the Director over the edge. And you are slowly getting at the truth of the Hansel and Gretel House fairy tale house that in moments of upset could become the House of Usher. But there was one house that gave you peace and security.

It was the brick palace, 3022a Kossuth in the heart of Old North St. Louis. I am honored to be a literary ambassador of the beloved Kielys and Malones, who frequented that place. They are now part of the Disadvantaged Royalty of North St. Louis who have returned to their home in the stars.

AUTHOR

I've tried to give the audience a few more bits and pieces of what they voted on, but it's time for the ending.

Would everyone please join me on stage?

They gather next to Iris.

I feel as though now I am able to bring this Finale to its close. All of you have opened my eyes to what I hesitate to call my unreliable narration.

An Unreliable narrator withholds key information from readers.

I certainly would not deceive, but the memoir of my life in the 1950s did fall short of many facts. I see that now, and I must do a better job in the light of this reality. My dear virtual family, I need to say this quick or I'll be full of tears. It's become obvious that I have been hiding an awful lot and using historical fiction to do it.

Secrets consumed the Malone family, so forgive me. And you were right, Iris; it *was* embarrassing to think that we were the talk of the block, the block being my entire outside world as a child. I don't have to go into detail about what may have been embarrassing. People have imaginations vivid enough to understand. What I do have to do is make an announcement.

IRIS

I don't think I want to hear this

The abduction scene may have been a subconscious wish to redo what happened in front of the mirror. The author addresses the virtual characters, but looks directly at the audience while she does. Perhaps it's another of her evasions from anything that seems just too much to bear.

AUTHOR

I'll just say this quickly to get through it. I'm stepping back from fiction for a while. I don't think it will be permanent, and of course I will always be thinking of you, but I have to keep seeking the stardust in me to stay close to the truth as every writer must. Maybe I will finally discover why I thought I needed to hide the real story of my life.

So long is the only thing I will say, not good-bye, because "these precious days" have meant more to me than you will ever know. You've been a blessing in my life and I wish you all the goodness that your next script has to offer. Let's remember each other.

I'll see you in my dreams.

The Director is physically shaking, his voice cracking as he tells the audience to meet at Fuzzies for a final toast and farewell. The virtuals wave to the Author as she picks up the frayed rope and begins to climb the ladder in hopes of making a clean break.

The curtain begins to fall but the scene becomes pandemonium. The place is in an uproar as the audience rushes the stage yelling things like, "We can't let you leave it all behind." The virtuals huddle under the large sign that the Author is scaling. The stagehands come out to try to keep the Author from falling off the ladder and the Director is calling security.

Chaos reigns and the Fourth Wall is holding but may crumble at any moment. It looks like a literary coup. Who will write Book VII, the Author, the Audience or the entire cast and crew? It may take a village and more than one genre to unwind out of this scene. By the way, which way is Fuzzies?

End of Play

DÉNOUEMENT INACHEVÉ

Thought I would give this walk out of historical fiction a French twist.

Dénouement is French for the final part of a story for which the treads of the narrative are pulled together.

In this case inachevé means it was not resolved.

But as Iris said I may have to "think again." I do know, however, that I am free to begin the story of the next pieces of my life in what Cleve would call PR, Pure Reality. Gosh I miss him already, but he's out there somewhere, wishing me well. I know my options are to fall off the ladder and crash right through the Fourth Wall, or chicken out and stay in the house of fiction.

Until I get to the decision point, I can only relish the five-book memoir that ended along with the 1950s, because PR, Pure Reality, began in the 1960s. It was then that a walk up Helen Avenue led me to Marillac Provincial House, and to my first job blocks away at The Army Mobility Equipment Command. In 1970 I married Greg, the best guy in the world, and all this within throwing distance of Helen Avenue.

I loved, worked, and studied my way through the '70s, and in 1980 received a master's degree from

Washington University that gave me the credentials I needed to begin teaching at Holy Cross Grade School, then St. Vincent's Orphan's Home, and St. Louis Community College as an adjunct professor in the English Department at night. By day I worked for Congressman William L. Clay, and in 1990 I joined the staff of the St. Louis County Executive.

In the 2000s my boundaries widened a bit when I began teaching at the City of St. Charles School District and later at the St. Charles Community College. Yes, most of my life happened with a few miles of the Hansel and Gretel House on Helen Avenue. My life has been neither cosmopolitan nor cloistered, but what it has been is fascinating.

Over time, I became a scribe of stardust words. They were the threads for everything I ever wrote as I sat in classrooms and then stood before them. Every job I ever had required that I write. So the stardust words grew into an empire of self-published books filled with goodness and joy that only words made of stardust can provide.

At some point I realized that stardust words were leading me down a road of creativity. But creating words made of stardust is difficult as M. Scott Peck confirmed in the first sentence of *The Road Less Traveled, "Life is difficult.*" Luckily, I had the influence of living inside a laugh, so the old tension and conflict of the Hansel and Gretel house was offset by an inner joy. I always found a happy way out of any sad thoughts that did linger, because my ticket out of them was the words I wrote. They always took me away.

Getting to now, I must say I've enjoyed the house of fiction that sheltered me during most of my writing career. I suppose now I'm running away from home, but just for a while. I'm not leaving forever. I will be back, because I couldn't bear to say a final goodbye to the place where stardust words sheltered me. The countless hours I spent creating characters inside the house of fiction is something I'll always be grateful for. No, I won't abandon the place, but I also know I have to pursue new trails.

Jumping off the Stardust Trail that meandered through the memoir series will let me find new ways of revealing more about my life and the life of fiction itself. Although it's historical fiction, I'm glad I stuck with the play, and I look forward to writing a non-fiction narration that tells the story of my next pursuit. This flexibility could extend my contract for Book VII, or crash through the Fourth Wall. Yikes!

You're thinking… she's still hooked up with fiction because she refers to things like stardust words and virtual characters like Cleve. You could be right, but here's the difference. I am one who truly *really* believes in the power of stardust to influence the words I write which makes me a cosmotheorist. As Myay would say a big "c" word. They are filled with as much stardust as I am and they move my ideas. They power the direction signals that tell me which way to proceed.

Until stardust is proven to have no force within us, I'll stay a cosmotheorist. But I believe that stardust is an active force in us. I like the definition right out of Star Wars that the force is an energy field that binds the universe together. Yep, that's stardust. The origin is known, but its influence to bind words into meaning is as yet unknown. My stardust words are not profound, but give them a chance and they will find their way into your heart.

I know the force is in me when I write and hear that my words changed a heart in a small but good way. So, for me stardust words are very real. I believe they will have the same power of amazement and discovery in non-fiction as they did in the house of fiction. The House of Fiction did give me hours of peace. By the way, the *House of Fiction* is the title of one of the most interesting books I've ever read. It's about the great houses of literature, but I can't imagine any of them were as intriguing as Auntie's Palace of Brick.

Escaping the Hansel and Gretel House on Helen Avenue in Jennings, and making my way to my aunt's brick palace in North St. Louis was a weekly goal of my childhood, but goals fade and it turned out to be only a temporary fix.

The palace stood quite regally well into the 1960s, but it didn't last. When Auntie got too old to keep the place up and host us every weekend we found a little place in Jennings near us for her and my Uncle Johnie to live. I visited them there until their deaths. That was around the time the house of fiction took me in.

Motif such as that of a house is a recurring image or symbol.

My need for a house that would shelter me brings to mind how good it was of the Mulanphy family to provide shelter for the Irish immigrants and others in North St. Louis to have the Mulanphy House to call home. Theirs was a goodness and generosity like that of the people who raised me. Immigrants stayed there until they could get a job and save enough rent money for a row house like my mother lived in on Biddle Street when she was young.

The Mulanphy House became a sacred shelter to many, like the house of fiction was to me. The house of fiction gave me space to happily create characters that I know were sent into the pages of literature to spread goodwill to their literary corner of the world.

If I fall off the ladder and crash through the wall, I'll pack my bags with stardust words and head out to non-fiction's glaring light of public scrutiny. But, as Maureen O'Hara said, "I want my things about me." I only want one thing though, a mirror that reflects Greg, the Malones and Kielys, virtual characters, and former students standing beneath me for I've always reached for the stars while standing on their shoulders.

As for the last scene of the play and which way the story will go, well I'm the author who believes writing is the one way to see evolution in action so it remains to be seen. As Myay would say, "Get it."

Inspiration from the Text of the The City Brick Memoir Series

Book I
The Shelter of Trees

It's about being excited and passionate about ordinary things that can bring on a kind of drama when growing up into a new self. Also, it's about the happiness that comes from all things fantastic when the world is new. This is the fascination of being young.

Book II
The Shelter of Cool Confidence

It's about finding ways to build the confidence to say what you think and write it truthfully. It's about keeping humor right inside your imagination as you write, and learning all you can from others to make life easier. It's about searching for your creativity and applying by taking up the vocation of creative writing. This is the independence of being confident.

Book III
Paper The Moon With Stardust Words

It's about digging in to whatever you choose to do in life. If it's writing, to follow up with the creative spirit in you and really become engaged with words. There is a science to the use of words; there is an art to the placement of words. There's a perception to where words can take you, and there's an elation of arriving at a good place. This is the accomplishment of being skilled.

Book IV
The Star Kingdom Trail

It's about the one journey in life that leads to a destination that will make you happy. It's about the spirit of pursuit that brings an element of excitement and makes you want to continue. It's about experiencing the goodness and the joy that comes from realizing there's love and support along the way. This is the fruit of staying optimistic.

Book V
The Shelter of City Brick

It's about connecting to life in all its forms and the neighborhood is an important one. It's about residing in the space between the eyes and book in a place called the imagination. It's especially important for a neighborhood like North St. Louis where The Disadvantaged Royalty relied on relationships with neighbors. This is the reward of loving.

List of Literary Devices and Techniques

WORKS CITED:

Bunton, M. Catherine. City Brick, St. Louis. years Series, Books I – V

https://www.scientificamerican.com/article/carl-sagans-star-stuff-made-real/

https://en.wikipedia.org/wiki/Wikipedia:Text_of_the_Creative_Commons_Attribution-ShareAlike_4.0_International_License

https://dynamic.stlouis-mo.gov/history/

https://www.google.com/

https://literary-devices.com/

https://www.sparknotes.com/lit/

https://www.supersummary.com/

https://en.wikipedia.org/wiki/Reader's_guide

City Brick, Microsoft Package with free Microsoft Designer and Copilot

Kroeger, Diana Beresford. To Speak For Trees. Timber Press, 2019.

Toole, John Kennedy. *GradeSaver* LLC. USA 2006.

Richardson, Phyllis. House of Fiction. Unbound, 2017.Famous Houses Book

***

www.ingramcontent.com/pod-product-compliance
Lightning Source LLC
LaVergne TN
LVHW010603110826
845149LV00003B/758

* 9 7 9 8 9 9 3 6 7 0 6 1 4 *